Shot at and Missed:

Mid-Acts Dispensationalism Fires Back.

Terence D. McLean

Discerning The Times Publishing

Shot at and Missed: Mid-Acts Dispensationalism Fires Back
Copyright © 2009 Discerning the Times Publishing

All rights reserved.

No part of this book may be reproduced or transmitted in any form or by any means, electronic or mechanical, digital or analog, including photo-copying, or placement in any information storage or retrieval system, multi-media, or internet system, without express written permission from the publisher:

Discerning the Times Publishing
Post Office Box 181
Greentown, IN 46936-0181

All scripture quotations in this book are taken from God's perfectly preserved words, the King James Bible.

ISBN-13: 978-0-9789863-4-6
ISBN-10: 0-9789863-4-2

Table of Contents

Preface   5

Launching the Debate   9

The "in Christ before me" Argument   29

When Did the Body Begin?   35

Blowing Up the Whole System   60

The Summation   76

Epilogue —
Peter Ruckman's Letter, Alexandrian Creed, and Bio   85

Preface

Opposition to Mid-Acts Pauline dispensationalism comes from all corners.

Denominations oppose Pauline doctrines of right division because were all believers to become Mid-Acts and Pauline, each denomination would fold like the house of cards that it is.

Ignorant Christians oppose Pauline principles of right division because they are afraid of the unknown.

Few who oppose Mid-Acts Pauline dispensationalism are more bellicose and belligerent in declaring that opposition than is Dr. Peter S. Ruckman; and two of Dr. Ruckman's own statements explain why he is so very vocal and vociferous.

Dr. Ruckman likes to say that if something does not make sense, there is a buck in it for somebody, and more often than not he would be right in that assessment. And it does not make sense for Dr. Ruckman, who calls many of his followers "dumb-thump Baptists" and says "the first person to get saved the way you got saved was the Ethiopian eunuch" to decry dispensational thinking. No doubt those "dumb-thump Baptists" buy Dr. Ruckman's books and pay him to preach; and so, there is a buck in it.

Dr. Ruckman also likes to say that when a person finds out he is wrong about something, that person will not admit the error if either his reputation or his income depends upon that wrong thing, even though he has learned that he is wrong. For example, Dr. Ruckman knows there is one baptism in this dispensation yet he accepts two, realizing full well that his ability to have his church and his ministry depends upon having a tank of tepid water at the front of his auditorium.

But while the water in the baptistery may be tepid, Dr. Ruckman's hatred for Mid-Acts dispensationalism has always been red hot; and his booklet, <u>Hyperdispensationalism,</u> is perhaps his most fiery attack.

Dr. Ruckman has an earned doctorate from a notable University, is a most prolific author, clearly is an accomplished Bible teacher and a most staunch defender of the King James Bible; and so his opposition to Mid-Acts dispensationalism deserves a carefully considered response.

To make certain that Dr. Ruckman's teachings are not misrepresented or taken out of context, I asked him for permission to use his booklet within this book, permission which Dr. Ruckman graciously granted and for which I am grateful.

Since Dr. Ruckman's booklet, <u>Hyperdispensationalism,</u> is a scathing no-holds-barred attack on my Mid-Acts dispensational beliefs, there are times when my responses are somewhat acerbic. That said, my responses are intended to be professional and not personal, doctrinal and not divisive, beneficial and not banal.

The attack on Mid-Acts Pauline dispensationalism in Dr. Ruckman's booklet must be answered, however, for the benefit of new believers and for those who would preach and teach according to the revelation of the mystery. My answer to Dr. Ruckman's having taken his best shot at what I believe is that I have been shot at by one of the best, but he missed.

Dr. Ruckman's words from his booklet appear within this book indented in the serif Times New Roman font and my words in response are in the sans serif Zurich font you have been reading here. Where you see bold letters or italicized words used in Dr. Ruckman's text, those would be his emphasis, not mine. Errors in his booklet are noted with (sic).

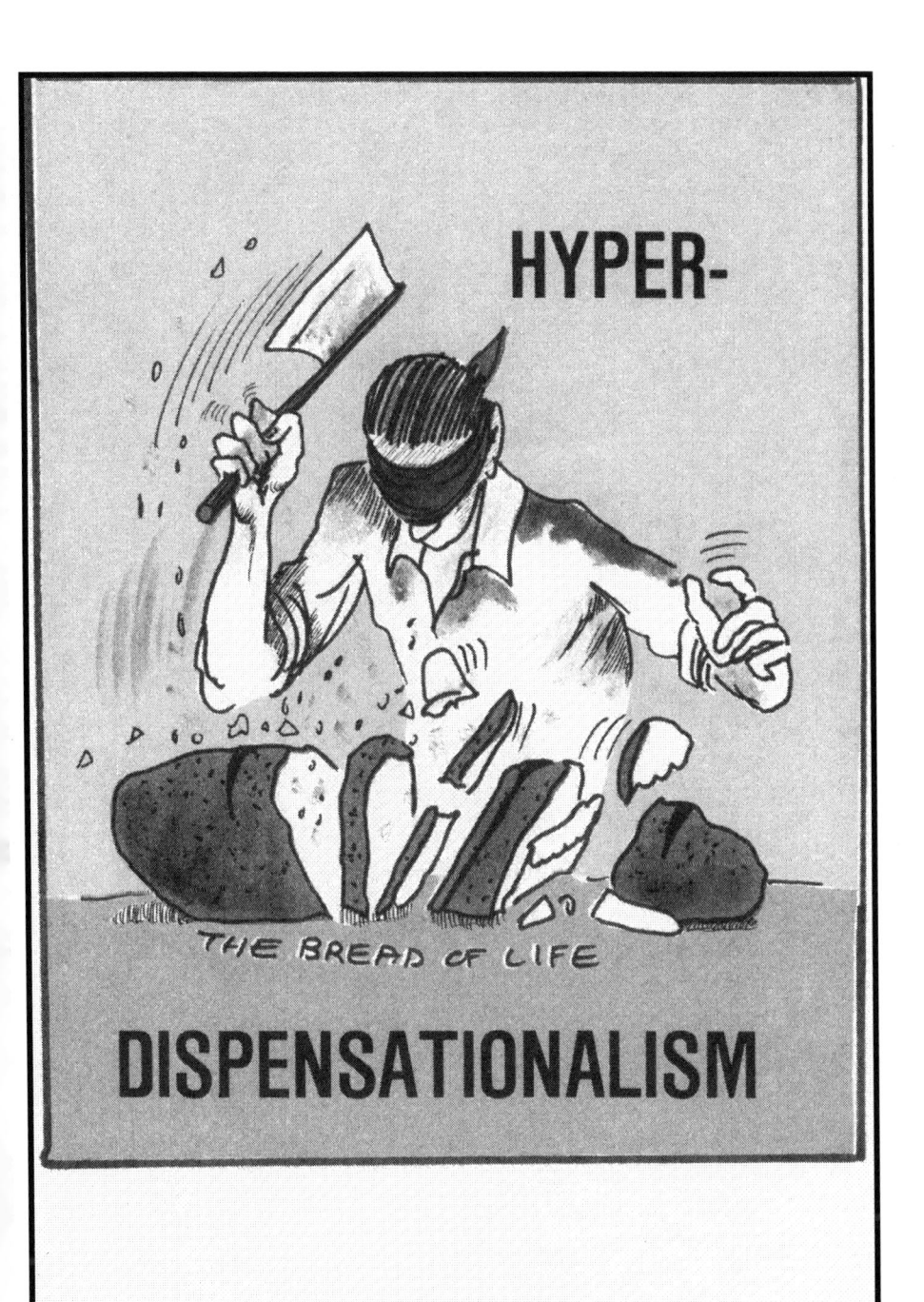

Depicted above is the cover of Dr. Ruckman's booklet.

Also, in the back of this book you will find Dr. Ruckman's letter to me granting permission to use his booklet; and his most considerable credentials are listed as well.

So with that you are ready to read on and decide for yourself if Dr. Ruckman hit his mark or if we Mid-Acts Pauline dispensationalists were:

Shot at and Missed.

Now, Mid-Acts Dispensationalism fires back

Launching the Debate

Dr. Peter S. Ruckman begins:

In this study I am going to discuss a fundamental heresy called *ultra-dispensationalism* or *hyper-dispensationalism*. I say "heresy" among Fundamentalists because this is a heresy that is taught by Bible Believing people. People who *believe* their Bible have their heresies exactly like unsaved people have theirs. The thing I am about to talk about is as much a "heresy" as the teaching of John Calvin on sprinkling babies or as much a heresy as the teaching of the Seventh Day Adventists or the Jehovah's's Witnesses.

Firstly, people who call Mid-Acts Pauline dispensationalism either "hyper" or "ultra" do so to disparage the concept with pejorative prefixes.

That, however is not a big deal when compared to being lumped in with Seventh Day Adventists or Jehovah's Witnesses. We who are Mid-Acts Pauline dispensationalists hold to the deity of the Lord Jesus Christ and have trusted His blood to pay for our sins, unlike the JW or SDA.

Frankly, Dr. Ruckman undoubtedly knows better and is attempting to propagandize using "guilt by association." But no Mid-Acts Pauline dispensationalist would ever, in any way, be associated with the Seventh Day Adventist or the Jehovah Witnesses, and he knows it.

In fairness to Dr. Ruckman, it must be said that not a few dispensationalists are Calvinists; and while none of them would ever sprinkle a baby, the percentage of Calvinistic dispensationalists is probably no more than the percentage of Calvinistic Baptists. That would be why Dr. Ruckman singles out baby sprinkling as the heresy to which he would compare dispensationalism, and so it is not difficult to see that what he is doing is little more than name-calling.

In the spirit of full disclosure, my position is anti-Calvinistic and anti-Armenian: not either/or but neither/nor.

Ultra-dispensationalism, or what we call "hyper-dispensationalism," is built upon the idea that since the Bible tells us to **"Study to shew thyself approved unto God, a workman that needeth not to be ashamed, rightly dividing the word of truth,"** that the word of God has proper *divisions* which we must observe, and if we get things out of placement in these divisions, then we are teaching false doctrine. There is some truth in this statement.

"Some truth" indeed. And while it is interesting that there are quite a few Baptists who consider Dr. Ruckman to be an "ultra" or "hyper" dispensationalist himself, we can be thankful that he sees at least "some truth" in what we believe. That is more respect than I would expect him to grant a heresy as terrible as something he would lump in with the Seventh Day or the JW, but that's just me.

It is perfectly apparent that the Old and New Testaments are two different 'dispensations," and it is perfectly apparent that the instructions for one do not match the instructions for the other. This is very manifest, of course, in such simple matters as the matter of *diet.* In Leviticus 11 we are told that certain meats are not to be eaten. In 1 Timothy 4:1-5 we are told that they certainly *can* be eaten if they are prayed about before they are eaten. This disparagement in accounts (or this difference in instructions) can only be accounted for dispensationally. When we read the Book of Acts we see the transition in Acts 10 where Simon Peter is taught that he should not call anything that God hath cleansed "common or unclean."

Additionally, Adam and Eve were instructed to be vegetarians in Genesis 1:29 and Noah was told he could kill and eat anything that moved in Genesis 9:3. Further, that would mean that God's instructions in Genesis 1:29 and Leviticus 11 would be "doctrines of devils" were they in place at the same time as 1 Timothy 4:1-5.

But while Dr. Ruckman failed to point out there were two dietary programs in place prior to the institution of the Old Testament, I am thankful for his admission that dispensational distinctives exist and are important. What we have for dinner, to use Dr. Ruckman's own words, "can only be accounted for dispensationally."

Peter in Acts 10, as Dr. Ruckman suggests, is in transition; but Dr. Ruckman fails to see that Peter never does understand Paul (II Peter 3:16) and that Peter and Paul go their separate ways (Galatians 2:7-9).

> This is very important because it shows that the *Book of Acts* is a *transitional period* that takes us from the Old Testament to the New Testament.

And the same people who got the Old Testament get the New Testament (Jeremiah 31: 31, Hebrews 8:8-10, Romans 15:8); and we are part of neither (Ephesians 2:12). The Bible does not contain simply the Old and New Testaments: there is a third item, and it is not the concordance or the maps in the back. There is the dispensation of the grace of God according to the revelation of the mystery.

However, at this point Dr. Ruckman says some accurate things about Calvinists and Campbellites, no doubt for the sake of his own credibility. With all of the wrong things he has already said and will be saying about dispensationalism, it is not surprising that he would attempt to gain some credibility by saying some truthful things while wrongly throwing dispensationalists into the mix.

> For this reason some of the greatest heretics who ever lived base their teaching on the Book of Acts. For example, there is not a *Church of Christ* preacher in the United States that doesn't base his entire system on Acts 2:38. And *Calvin* can be found fooling around in the Book of Acts where we read in Acts 13:48, "**...as many as were ordained to eternal life**

believed." That isn't all. Every *Postmillennial preacher* in the world can be found in Acts 2 where he will be found insisting that the Lord Jesus Christ is now on *David's* throne reigning over David's kingdom. The Book of Acts, then, is a dangerous place for anybody to rest doctrinally, and just as the Campbellite or Church of Christ preacher rests on his water baptism for salvation, so the ultra-dispensationalists get rid of water baptism altogether and make as much an issue of it as the Church of Christ preachers do.

However, no Mid-Acts dispensationalist gets rid of water baptism based on the book of Acts. For Dr. Ruckman to get away with that wrong statement requires that his readers neither search the scriptures nor study what we Mid-Acts dispensationalists actually believe.

I am going to talk about these things from personal experience, having dealt firsthand with several dozen of these people in several different states under all kinds of conditions. Let me, from the beginning, make some very simple statements which we will prove as we go on.

Having dealt with more than several dozen Baptists under all kinds of conditions, we will endeavor to set the good Doctor straight as he blends personal experience with his doctrinal dilemma.

The first statement is that the man who subscribes to hyper-dispensationalism is as hung up on *non-baptism* as any Campbellite preacher who ever lived is hung up on *water baptism*.

This bodacious statement is really a hoot when you consider who it is that has named his church, his bookstore, his newsletter and probably his German Shepherd after John the Baptist and the water ceremony of baptism.

Baptism is not even an issue to the Mid-Acts dispensationalist because we could care less. If you were sprinkled matters to Dr. Ruckman and his Baptist friends, but not to us. If you were baptized in a different denomination matters to Dr. Ruckman's Baptist Brider friends, but not to us. If you had a wet finger trace the shape of a cross on your forehead, Dr. Ruckman's cronies would say that would not qualify as baptism because they would care; we do not.

Every saved Mid-Acts dispensationalist has been baptized by God the Holy Spirit into the body of Christ. The ones with the hang up would not be us but would be those who call themselves Baptists, their very name evidencing their water fixation.

> As a matter of fact, the more you watch these people through the years the more you realize that they have a neurotic obsession with this phase of their Bible learning.

This from a man who called me a "drycleaner" in his newsletter published by his Baptist church. What a hoot. If "drycleaner" is a pejorative term, does that mean Dr. Ruckman and his Baptist church think that they were cleaned by getting wet? (Someone get the dictionary so the Baptists Dr. Ruckman calls his "dumb-thump Baptists" can look up "pejorative").

> The all-important thing to the hyper-dispensationalist is to *get rid of Baptist churches*. These people are obsessed with this to the point of fanaticism, and that won't be hard to prove as we go along.

Obviously Dr. Ruckman is in error on this point as we dispensationalists would not single out Baptists: it would be our desire to get rid of all denominations.

For Dr. Ruckman, however, his statement is true to him because of his personal experience, as he suffered a very nasty church split at the hands of dispensationalists who tore up his Baptist church rather than just leaving graciously.

> They get so obsessed with this non-water bit that it is all they can think about, eat, breathe, drink or sleep. And no matter where you find these people, in any state or under any condition, they are busy trying to get members to leave *Baptist* churches.

It may be that more Baptists see the truth of mid-Acts dispensationalism than people in other denominations because, generally speaking, Baptist people know more Bible and are closer to the truth than are many others.

To say we have a fixation over "this non-water bit" is hilarious in the face of the fact that the Baptists have named their whole outfit after the "water bit" as pointed out earlier. Baptism is not our issue as we could care less: what's done is done and would be water under the bridge, so to speak.

> I don't know of a single exception to the rule in the cases I have known through the years.

Dr. Ruckman's personal knowledge may be considerable, but it is personal and it is not all inclusive. In my personal experience, I have seen members of the World Wide Church of God, Church of God Anderson, Church of God Cleveland, Apostolics, Methodists, Presbyterians, Roman Catholics, Church of Christ as well as Baptists convert to mid-Acts dispensationalism.

> Their ministry has revolved around convincing Baptists that they did the wrong thing when they got baptized in water.

Baloney. Tithing, maybe, but not baptism.

> The problem comes up: How does this fit into the program of hyper-dispensationalism? Well, it is real simple, but let me make my second statement first.

Let us not forget that the supposed problem is about how "non-baptism" fits into the program of hyper-dispensationalism; and we should find it to be real simple when Dr. Ruckman deals with the issue, which I continue to maintain is a non-issue. Let us hope just exactly what the good doctor is getting at becomes clear and let us not accuse him of being disingenuous just yet. Let's be more gracious than he, and give him the benefit of the doubt as he makes his second statement:

> My second statement is that the hyper-dispensationalist, exactly as the Campbellite, Seventh Day Adventist and Jehovah's Witness, has had to, from time to time, *adjust his theology* to meet the demands of scripture. And all these groups that suddenly charge out with this "great new thing" they have, this great new revelation, have one characteristic about them. As they come into conflict with real Bible-believing people who know the scriptures, *they have to keep adjusting their position closer and closer to the scriptures without abandoning their position.*

However, we are not "exactly as the Cambellite, Seventh Day Adventist and Jehovah's Witness" because we are saved and they are not.

Contrary to the way Dr. Ruckman makes it sound, the fact that there has been adjustment of dispensational theology to meet the demands of scripture would be a good thing would it not? It was not until Martin Luther and the Reformation that Pauline truth began to be rediscovered; and while more than four centuries have passed since then, there is always more to learn.

When did it become a bad thing to adjust to meet the demands of scripture? Answer: when either your income or your reputation precludes it or when there is a buck in it for someone: that's when.

> And so, when talking about "hyper-dispensationalism," at the very start I am going to tell you what these people believe.

That will be interesting...

> They will then deny everything I *say* they believe and produce the scriptures for their "circular reasoning." When they get through after six hours, you will find that they believe exactly what I told you they believe. *All heretics have what we call "circular reasoning."*

If scripture can be produced, in what sense would it be "circular reasoning?" Isn't it circular reasoning to agree there is just one baptism only to teach and practice two? Isn't it circular reasoning to make being a "drycleaner" an insult while agreeing that getting wet is not involved in salvation? Isn't it circular reasoning to say the so-called drycleaners have a water fixation when we mid-Acts dispensationalists stay dry while the Baptists have named their church in accordance with a water ceremony?

> It is a reasoning that begins with one verse and runs to another and runs to another and runs to another to complete a circle to get across something that is not true. You just try "cornering" one of these fellows one time on one verse and you will find that fellow will fly like the wind to the next verse. This is characteristic of all Campbellite preachers, all Jehovah's Witnesses, all Seventh Day Adventists, and it is very very true of hyper-Calvinists.

Hmmmm: beginning with one verse, then another and another and another and tying all the verses together would be connecting the dots rather than the Baptist proof text approach of collecting the dots, would it not? And why would that be a bad thing, exactly?

Once again, Dr. Ruckman tosses the saved dispensationalist into the same bucket as the unsaved Campbellite, Seventh Day and JW, his intent being then to kick that bucket and everyone in it. This is probably intended to scare his Baptist audience away from looking into mid-Acts dispensationalism; but it is clear his statements are hyperbole lacking intellectual integrity.

And for all his chest-beating, we still are waiting to be cornered and forced to run.

> In this booklet we are talking about *hyper-dispensationalists*. What is a hyper-dispensationalist? Well, the original position was stated by a man named Ethelbert Bullinger, who lived back in the nineteenth century and wrote *The Companion Bible*.

In point of fact, Bullinger was an Acts 28 dispensationalist and he was not the first nor is he representative of all dispensationalism.

If the reader of Dr. Ruckman's booklet does not know better, he might fall into the trap of painting all dispensationalists with Bullinger's errors. That would be like lumping Dr. Ruckman's Baptists in with the Free Will Baptists, Southern Baptists, Progressive Baptists, National Baptists, Conservative Baptists and the most remarkable Two Seed In The Spirit Predestinarian Baptists.

There are more flavors of Baptists than there are flavors of ice cream at the Piggly Wiggly, and to say they all believe the same would be dishonest. For Dr. Ruckman to suggest that all dispensationalists believe as Ethelbert Bullinger is both dishonest and ignorant; and Dr. Ruckman most certainly is not ignorant.

Not only that, before there was Bullinger there was John Nelson Darby; and contemporaneous with Bullinger was C. I. Scofield and Sir Robert Anderson. And before Darby and Bullinger and Scofield and Anderson, there was Paul, who said the dispensation of the grace of God was given by Christ to him to make known the revelation of the mystery.

In Dr. Ruckman's booklet, without having cornered anyone or really proven anything, his description of Bullinger's errors which follows is harsh, but reasonably accurate:

> Bullinger taught this: (1) That only the *prison epistles* written by Paul after the close of the Book of Acts could be considered as *doctrine* for the Christian; (2) That the Body found in the Book of Acts is *not* the Body of Christ mentioned in Ephesians 2 and 3; and (3) That the "mystery Body" Paul mentions in Ephesians 2 and 3 did not show up until *after the close of Acts 28.*

We who are mid-Acts dispensationalists disagree with Bullinger on these points as well. We know full well that Paul was separated unto the Gentiles to preach the one body from day one, which would have been Acts nine, as reported in

Acts 26:16-17:

> "But rise, and stand upon thy feet: for I have appeared unto thee for this purpose, to make thee a minister and a witness both of these things which thou hast seen, and of those things in the which I will appear unto thee; Delivering thee from the people, and from the Gentiles, unto whom now I send thee,"

It would also be good to point out that Bullinger died before completion of the Companion Bible, that Charles Welch completed that work, and that neither Bullinger nor Welch was a King James Bible believer.

As dispensational thinking matured and become more nuanced, the mid-Acts position emerged as the sound position. Dr. Ruckman said this was a matter of our dispensational theology changing because of the demands of scripture, and that also would be accurate and is a good thing.

> With this, Bullinger got fouled up on the prepositions in Ephesians 1 about "all things" being in Christ and finally wound up proposing *universal salvation for everybody, including the devil.* Strangely enough, Ephesians 1 contains the proof text for hyper-Calvinism.

Actually, some of the positions being ascribed to Bullinger are positions taken by Welch; but irrespective of that, no mid-Acts dispensationalist would agree with universalism.

> So, we can learn something.

Yes, we can learn that Dr. Ruckman is attempting to paint all dispensationalists with the same brush, that he is attempting to hang the errors of the Acts 28 dispensationalists on mid-Acts dispensationalists; and that is disingenuous if not dishonest.

Dr. Ruckman has said that the first person in the Bible to get saved the way that you and I got saved was the eunuch in Acts chapter eight. What actually happened in Acts 8 was Philip told the eunuch about Israel's Messiah from Isaiah 53 and by believing in the Messiah as found in the prophesies for Israel, the eunuch joined the Little Flock of Israel.

Although Dr. Ruckman fails to respect Pauline doctrine as being distinct, he is rather close to getting it right as Acts eight is close to being mid-Acts. But close, as we all know, only counts in horseshoes and hand grenades.

We do respect that Dr. Ruckman has identified himself as believing differently than the Baptist Briders that constitute much of his audience: but the gospel of the grace of God is never mentioned in Acts 8.

Further, while it would be wrong for us to believe all Baptists are the same, it is equally wrong for Dr. Ruckman and the Baptists to call all dispensationalists "hyper" and dismiss us all based on the errors of a few.

> We can learn that Ephesians 1 is a very dangerous place to be fooling around in if you are unlearned and unstable. Both hyper-Calvinism and hyper-dispensationalism have their foundation in the Book of Ephesians and both of them use references to verses in the Book of Acts to prove their particular position.

Actually, the "all things" of Ephesians chapter one is not all that difficult:

> *"That in the dispensation of the fulness of times he might gather together in one all things in Christ, both which are in heaven, and which are on earth; even in him:"*
> *- Ephesians 1:10:*

The dispensation of the fulness of times was not included among the seven dispensations that C. I. Scofield or John Nelson Darby or Peter S.

Ruckman, for that matter, ever taught. Very simply, in that future dispensation of the fullness of times, the two things that constitute the "all things" in the verse, are combined in one in Christ. The two things involve that which is in heaven (which is the body of Christ) and that which is on earth (which is Israel's kingdom church).

All the saved from all dispensations end up in Christ: not universalism but rather the Bible description of a dispensation Dr. Ruckman and most others simply missed because of their tradition-bound Baptist thinking.

Next, Dr. Ruckman actually makes several mid-Acts dispensational points:

> The position changes a bit under *J. C. O'Hare* (the radio preacher out of Chicago). He backslid from Bullinger's position because of a number of things. First of all was the very embarrassing (and very *obvious*) thing which was pointed out to him by some Bible-believing Baptist that 1 Corinthians 12 is already dealing with the "mystery Body" and the members of the Body, and it says clearly **"For by one Spirit are we all baptized into one body...."** This epistle was written *during the Acts period* to converts of the Corinthian church. So, O'Hare backslid and decided that the Body of Christ began in Acts 18. Acts 18 was dealing with the Corinthian church and this "saved face" for the dispensationalists temporarily because they had the "Body of Christ" beginning in Acts 18 during the Acts period and yet they still could dump the water baptism. The *last cases* they found of water baptism in the Book of Acts were in Acts 18 and 19 and, by dispensationally treating the passage in Acts 19 that dealt with the baptism of Apollos' converts (vv. 1-7), they could say that water baptism *ended* in Acts 18; therefore, the Body of Christ *began* in Acts 18.

While O'Hair (correct spelling) did not place the start of the body of Christ in Acts 18, he did move away from the Acts 28 position of Welch and Bullinger and gravitated toward mid-Acts.

Paul did some baptizing, as we all know; and so for it to be true that Christ sent him not to baptize but the preach the gospel, it would be clear that either Paul was disobedient to Christ or more likely that Christ sent Paul not to baptize at a later point after a subsequent meeting.

And once again, the same Dr. Ruckman who says that the dumb-thump Baptists are stuck in the mud right where C. I. Scofield left them in 1917 turns around and disparages advancements in dispensational thinking.

> This is typical of the heretic who doesn't know what he is talking about. He makes his direct statement and then has to adjust and readjust and readjust to meet the demands of the scripture.

Now how did we get to this point?

Firstly, we have to buy into all dispensationalists agreeing with the errors of Bullinger and Welch and then we have to think it is a wrong thing to adjust to meet the demands of scripture. For Dr. Ruckman to do this, as a Baptist having friends who think Christ was a Baptist because John baptized Jesus into membership into a Baptist church, is stunning.

> And, of course, the deliberate choice of Acts 18 as the starting place shows exactly what we are dealing with. We are dealing with a bunch of people who are devoted to getting rid of water baptism in *any* form.

What J. C. O'Hair might have said is no more representative of mid-Acts dispensationalism than that which might have been said by Welch, Darby, Scofield or Bullinger. Dr. Ruckman is attempting to paint all dispensationalists with the same brush, and this is just as wrong as it would be to identify all Baptists with Billy Graham or Pat Robertson.

And much more important than getting rid of water baptism would be getting the gospel right and seeing souls saved.

Unlike the Baptists, we dispensationalists know that repenting does not mean turning and that asking Jesus into one's heart is meaningless blather. Getting rid of the Baptist pattern of teaching that Romans 10:9-10 or John 1:12 are the plan of salvation would mean more to us with a heart for souls than draining the water from one thousand baptistries.

The Baptist "Every head bowed, every eye closed, no one looking around" would be three lies to start with.

"Come down front and give your heart to the Lord Jesus," as if Jesus can't make it to the back of the auditorium and making it very difficult for shy or embarrassed church members, deacons and preachers to get saved, is nothing less than crowd manipulation.

"Pray the sinners prayer: Lord be merciful to me, a sinner;" but why should the Lord be merciful? How about presenting the gospel?

When I met the man called the Prince of Preachers, B. R. Lakin, he told me that he thought two thirds of Baptist church members would land in hell. Dear old Vance Havner, in his eighties after six decades of preaching, told me he thought three quarters of Baptist church members would land in hell; and true to his always memorable ways of saying things, he told me "We might get more saved if we didn't baptize them and put them in the choir first."

Now follows more hyperbole at the expense of truth:

> Because of this, the fundamental, Bible-believing Baptist churches have as their worst theological opponents in this age the dispensationalists who follow the teaching of J. C. O'Hare, Baker, Cornelius Stam and Bullinger. Furthermore, when these men write of Independent Baptist churches, they write of them as churches that are "in bondage to tradition," churches that feel unfree to follow the teaching of structure, and churches that are afraid to "tell the truth" to their people.

We mid-Acts dispensationalists are not the theological opponents of saved people who teach salvation is by grace through faith in Christ's payment for our sins on the cross of Calvary. We may disagree on many things, but we do not oppose any saved person's serving Christ as best he knows how.

Of course we know that tithing is wrong and the Baptist doesn't, but that does not make us the worst theological opponent the Baptists have any more than does our knowing Sunday is not the "Christian Sabbath" or that Israel is born again, not us.

So-ever-what? That does not constitute any Baptist's worst theological opposition: that would be left to the Mormons or the JWs or the Seventh Day or the Apostolics, but not to us.

Dr. Ruckman knows how to tar and feather people he doesn't like; but we, graciously, will not respond in kind.

> These "dry cleaners" who follow this particular movement will come to your church and get in your church and draw away your young people into "Bible studies" (that is what Judge Rutherford and Pastor Russell called their students– *Bible* students) and then teach them that water baptism is not for them.

Here Dr. Ruckman has a point; and while we mid-Acts dispensaitonalists are correct to resent his lumping us in with Rutherford, Russell and the JWs once again, if we dispensationalists tear up a Baptist church, shame on us.

One Baptist fellow learned something about mid-Acts dispensationalism from me and asked me more and more questions, week after week. Finally one day he let it slip that he was using what he learned from me to confound the Sunday School teacher in his Baptist church and to tear up the class.

What a jerk!

He needed to get out of that Baptist church and start his own study group and grow that into a mid-Acts dispensational assembly.

What a jerk!

By going to the Baptist church, he was endorsing it; and then by doing what he did in the Sunday School class, he gave all mid-Acts dispensationalists a bad name.

What a jerk!

And those men who tore up Dr. Ruckman's Baptist church should be ashamed of themselves. They were jerks as well.

Now, it gets a bit more complicated:

> Continuing with the history of the matter, it was called to the attention of J. C. O'Hare the remarkable verse (which is perfectly apparent to anybody) in Acts 16 which states that the apostle Paul baptized converts *after* he knew about "the gospel of the grace of God."

This would mean that Paul knew the doctrine which Paul himself referred to three times as "my gospel," but that the Lord had yet to send Paul not to baptize, which is why I made that point earlier.

Since the truth is that we have no Acts 18 fixation or predilection, all Dr. Ruckman is doing here is beating the daylights out of a straw man. Paul gets saved in Acts 9 and the Lord Jesus sends Paul on his way right then, promising to teach Paul additional information later on.

> *Acts 26:16-17: But rise, and stand upon thy feet: for I have appeared unto thee for this purpose, to make thee a minister and a witness both of these things which thou hast seen, and of those things in the which I will appear unto thee; Delivering thee from the people, and from the Gentiles, unto whom now I send thee,*

Then, Dr. Ruckman really confounds things by what he says next:

> As a matter of fact, it is perfectly clear from Acts 15 that the "gospel of the grace of God" was known to all the apostles, for Simon Peter in Acts 15 says in verst 11, **"But we believe that through the grace of the Lord Jesus Christ we shall be saved, even as they."**

Actually, Peter's grace is not according to the gospel of grace but according to the gospel of prophecy, the gospel of the kingdom; but what Baptist knows that?

Peter did not preach the cross except as Israel's murder indictment, with Peter's attempting to prevent the Lord from going to the cross:

> *Matthew 16:21-22: From that time forth began Jesus to shew unto his disciples, how that he must go unto Jerusalem, and suffer many things of the elders and chief priests and scribes, and be killed, and be raised again the third day. Then Peter took him, and began to rebuke him, saying, Be it far from thee, Lord: this shall not be unto thee.*

Has any Baptist ever noticed that Peter, who had been preaching the gospel of the kingdom and water baptizing since Matthew 10, did not understand the cross and tried to prevent the Lord from going to Calvary?

Has any Baptist ever had it dawn on him or her that it is apparent the gospel of the kingdom must not have included the cross, but that the death, burial and resurrection constitute the gospel of the grace of God?

Has any Baptist ever figured out that the gospel of the kingdom and the gospel of the grace of God are different and that neither Peter nor Christ nor John the Baptist ever preached the gospel of the grace of God, only Paul, and that after the glorified Lord Jesus returned from heaven to reveal it?

Has any Baptist ever noticed that none of the apostles understood the cross and certainly none of them preached it or gloried in it:

> *Mark 9:31-32: For he taught his disciples, and said unto them, The Son of man is delivered into the hands of men, and they shall kill him; and after that he is killed, he shall rise the third day. But they understood not that saying, and were afraid to ask him.*

> *Luke 9:44-45: Let these sayings sink down into your ears: for the Son of man shall be delivered into the hands of men. But they understood not this saying, and it was hid from them, that they perceived it not: and they feared to ask him of that saying.*

> *John 20:9: For as yet they knew not the scripture, that he must rise again from the dead.*

Since we have not been cornered just yet, and since we have noted that Dr. Ruckman has made it a bad thing to adjust one's belief system to the Bible rather than the other-way-around, and since we will not be tricked into thinking Bullinger or O'Hair speaks for all dispensationalists, we find Dr. Ruckman to be straining at gnats as he continues:

> And plainly when the Philippian jailer asked, **"...What must I do to be saved?"** in Acts 16, Paul does not tell him to repent and be baptized in the name of Jesus Christ for the remission of sins. But rather he tells him, **"Believe on the Lord Jesus Christ, and thou shalt be saved...."** This is the teaching of Ephesians and Romans. So, it is perfectly apparent that in Acts 16, even though Paul knew the "gospel of the grace of God," *he still baptized the convert after getting him saved by*

grace through faith. After this was called to J. C. O'Hare's attention, Cornelius Stam and Baker took a step back further to Acts 9.

If the issue were water baptism, would not O'Hair, Stam and Baker have moved toward Acts 28 where there is less baptism rather than to Acts 9 where there is more? Of course they would have; but the issue is not baptism, as our Baptist friend would have us believe.

That which the good Baptist Doctor is failing to understand is that Paul's water baptism was in accordance with what Paul knew and had seen; but as soon as the Lord told him to stop, Paul stopped.

> *1 Corinthians 1:14: I thank God that I baptized none of you, but Crispus and Gaius;*

Paul had been baptized and he had done some baptizing, but that came to a screeching halt when the Lord told Paul differently in a meeting between the Lord and Paul subsequent to Acts 9.

> *1 Corinthians 1:17: For Christ sent me not to baptize, but to preach the gospel: not with wisdom of words, lest the cross of Christ should be made of none effect.*

At this point, Dr. Ruckman says some things that are simply wrong and then builds upon his error:

> *Now* this group is teaching that the "Body" began with *Paul.* This makes the Body of Christ from Acts 2 to Acts 9 one Body and the Body of Christ from Acts 9 on a different Body.

But there is no Body of Christ from Acts 2 to Acts 9: and Dr. Ruckman is counting on his reader's ignorance and the errors of tradition. We do not teach what he says we teach; just ask us rather than taking our opposition's word for it.

We know that Peter is talking to Jews in Acts 2 and Peter is preaching the last days of Israel as found in the book of Joel, not "the birthday of the church" as so many suppose.

> *Acts 2:16-17: But this is that which was spoken by the prophet Joel; And it shall come to pass in the <u>last days</u>, saith God, I will pour out of my Spirit upon all flesh: and your sons and your daughters shall prophesy, and your young men shall see visions, and your old men shall dream dreams:*

You could not find anything doctrinal for the church which is Christ's body in Acts 2 through 9 were I to give you a two week head start and a flashlight. If you think differently, please explain why you have not obeyed Acts 2:45 and 4:34-35.

> *Acts 2:45: And sold their possessions and goods, and parted them to all men, as every man had need.*

> *Acts 4:34-35: Neither was there any among them that lacked: for as many as were possessors of lands or houses sold them, and brought the prices of the things that were sold, And laid them down at the apostles' feet: and distribution was made unto every man according as he had need.*

The "In Christ Before Me" Argument

But, again, this got very embarrassing, for it was then called to their attention (and that is all I'm going to do with this booklet, just call it constantly to your attention so that you will wind up a Bible-believer instead of a hyper-dispensationalist) that some of Paul's kinfolk were "in Christ" *before Acts 9*. Notice the clearest statement of Paul about these matters in Romans 16. In Romans 16:7 he says, **"Salute Andronicus and Junia, my kinsmen, and my fellowprisoners, who are of note among the apostles, who also were in Christ before me."** This drove the dispensationalists up a tree so they finally came to the conclusion that you could be "in Christ" *without being in Christ's Body* (which is a very unique position to say the least).

Now, Dr. Ruckman and many others who oppose mid-Acts dispensationalism think that this is the "gotcha" to end all "gotchas," this business of being "in Christ" before Acts 9.

Ho hum.

Some are "in Christ" according to the prophetic program given to Israel and some of them were "in Christ" even before Calvary:

John 6:56: He that eateth my flesh, and drinketh my blood, dwelleth in me, and I in him.

John 15:5-7: I am the vine, ye are the branches: He that abideth in me, and I in him, the same bringeth forth much fruit: for without me ye can do nothing. If a man abide not in me, he is cast forth as a branch, and is withered; and men gather them, and cast them into the fire, and they are burned. If ye abide in me, and my words abide in you, ye shall ask what ye will, and it shall be done unto you.

Every saved person from any dispensation ends up "in Christ," but we do not all get there the same way. Why, Peter and his Acts 2 through 9 crowd do not even have a present possession of

God's grace as do we; and they won't have it until Christ returns to kingdom Israel.

1 Peter 1:13: Wherefore gird up the loins of your mind, be sober, and hope to the end for the grace that is to be brought unto you at the revelation of Jesus Christ;

Acts 3:19-21: Repent ye therefore, and be converted, that your sins may be blotted out, when the times of refreshing shall come from the presence of the Lord; And he shall send Jesus Christ, which before was preached unto you: Whom the heaven must receive until the times of restitution of all things, which God hath spoken by the mouth of all his holy prophets since the world began.

And while we are at it, has any Baptist noticed the words "since the world began" in the verse just above? Peter says very clearly that what he is preaching in the Acts 2 through 9 time frame is that which had been spoken by the mouth of all the holy prophets "since the world began." Note Paul preaches that which had been hidden "since the world began:"

Romans 16:25: Now to him that is of power to stablish you according to my gospel, and the preaching of Jesus Christ, according to the revelation of the mystery, which was kept secret since the world began,

Those two things cannot be the same, which means of course, that Dr. Ruckman's first error was to see only the old and new testaments in his Bible and to fail to recognize the Body of Christ as being separate from either.

We mid-Acts dispensationalists are neither Old Testament Israel nor are we New Testament Israel: we are the "Church of What's Happening Now!"

> The expression "in Christ" is a Pauline expression that deals with the "mystery" of the Body.

Now isn't that interesting: "in Christ" is said to be a Pauline expression, yet his argument depends on the doctrine not being Pauline. Doc, you can't have it both ways.

> Yet these people could not allow anybody to be "in Christ" *before Paul* (Acts 9) even though Paul says, **"...who also were in Christ before me."**

Actually, what we would say is that people "in Christ" before Paul were "in Christ" according to the prophetic program given to Israel. After Paul and the revelation of the mystery, we now are "in Christ" according to that mystery program and the changes that come with it.

> So, because of this, the last adjustment these hypocrites have made has been to say that the Body of Christ was in the *mind* of God before Acts 9 but was not in *reality* until after it was revealed to Paul.

It would have been helpful for Dr. Ruckman to have provided a reference to who it was that said the Body was in the mind of God before Acts 9 but not a reality, because this actually sounds as if Dr. Ruckman is accusing dispensationalists of having the same logical error that Dr. Ruckman himself espouses.

It is Dr. Ruckman who says that the Body of Christ began at the cross but nobody knew it. This is the convoluted logic Dr. Ruckman holds to, and is amazingly similar to the convoluted logic he ascribes to dispensationalists.

The fact would be that the revelation of the mystery was known by the Godhead before the foundation of the world, not just before Acts 9.

> *Ephesians 3:9 And to make all men see what is the fellowship of the mystery, which from the beginning of the world*

hath been hid in God, who created all things by Jesus Christ:

Ephesians 1:3-4 Blessed be the God and Father of our Lord Jesus Christ, who hath blessed us with all spiritual blessings in heavenly places in Christ: According as he hath chosen us in him before the foundation of the world, that we should be holy and without blame before him in love:

Romans 16:25 Now to him that is of power to stablish you according to my gospel, and the preaching of Jesus Christ, according to the revelation of the mystery, which was kept secret since the world began,

Colossians 1:26 Even the mystery which hath been hid from ages and from generations, but now is made manifest to his saints:

1 Timothy 1:8-11 But we know that the law is good, if a man use it lawfully; Knowing this, that the law is not made for a righteous man, but for the lawless and disobedient, for the ungodly and for sinners, for unholy and profane, for murderers of fathers and murderers of mothers, for manslayers, For whoremongers, for them that defile themselves with mankind, for menstealers, for liars, for perjured persons, and if there be any other thing that is contrary to sound doctrine; According to the glorious gospel of the blessed God, which was committed to my trust.

While I know of no dispensationalist who has ever said that the Body of Christ was in the mind of God before Acts 9 but not a reality until after it was revealed to Paul, would not the point actually be that it became a practical reality after it was revealed to Paul and that it was of no practical value prior to that revelation?

Regardless of whether the issue is there being a Body of Christ starting at the cross with no one knowing, or, there being a Body of Christ before Acts 9 with no one knowing, would not the most important element be that no one knew? And if no one knew, how would anyone have known to trust Christ by grace through faith rather than keeping the law and enduring to the end?

Dr. Ruckman's argument is a straw man to which we put a match by thinking the matter through.

> By doing this, they have switched back to Bullinger's old position and have gotten away with it by saying that the *Body did not actually begin with Paul* but that sometime in the Book of Acts there was a *gradual transition* to the Body as the mystery was revealed. This is the baloney you are going to get from the "hypers" today and, for this reason, we are going to make "short shrift" of them and pin the thing right down.

Dr. Ruckman does not tell us who comprises the "they", these people who have switched back to Bullinger, but my guess would be Pastor E. C. Moore, a preacher who also lives in Dr. Ruckman's home town of Pensacola. The fact is Pastor Moore has always leaned toward Acts 28 and it is true that some of Pastor Moore's followers call themselves mid-Acts while they lean toward Acts 28 as well; but none of these personal things really matter. Dr. Ruckman is saying that we mid-Acts dispensationalists are guilty of teaching that there was a gradual transition to the Body as the mystery was revealed.

Not so. While it is clear that Christ did not say everything Christ would ever say to Paul in one sitting, you will not hear from us that there was a gradual transition into the presence of the Body.

> *Acts 26:16-17: But rise, and stand upon thy feet: for I have appeared unto thee for this purpose, to make thee a minister and a witness both of these things which thou hast seen, and of those things in the which I will appear unto thee; Delivering thee from the people, and from the Gentiles, unto whom now I send thee,*

> *Galatians 1:15: But when it pleased God, who separated me from my mother's womb, and called me by his grace,*

Paul was only separated from his mother's womb the one time; but Christ did promise subsequent appearances to Paul after Acts 9, at which times Christ promised to impart to Paul additional "things."

There were to be visits and visions from the Lord, and there were; but Paul was sent to the Gentiles from Acts 9; and by Acts 13 Paul was saying things very grace-like:

> *Acts 13:38-39: Be it known unto you therefore, men and brethren, that through this man is preached unto you the forgiveness of sins: And by him all that believe are justified from all things, from which ye could not be justified by the law of Moses.*

Nine, thirteen: sort of in the middle. Clearly not 18 or 28 and undefined gradualism.

But at this point, Dr. Ruckman is counting on the ignorance of his followers and their willingness to oppose Pauline mid-Acts dispensationalism, because at this point Dr. Ruckman rides in on the back of his straw man with another "gotcha" to end all "gotchas."

When Did the Body Begin?

We are going to get our hand right on the issue.

The issue is: *When did the "Body" start?* That is the issue and there is no ducking it. It is true that these hypocrites will run to some other verses to prove the "mystery of the revelation" in order to sidetract (sic) you from locating when the Body started. But the issue has always been *when did the Body start.*

Let us cut to the chase here: the Body of Christ started with Paul, who was the last man to see Christ:

1 Corinthians 15:8: And last of all he was seen of me also, as of one born out of due time.

And Paul was the first and serves as the pattern for subsequent believers:

1 Timothy 1:16: Howbeit for this cause I obtained mercy, that in me first Jesus Christ might shew forth all longsuffering, for a pattern to them which should hereafter believe on him to life everlasting.

The Body of Christ was formed in the mind of God before the foundation of the world and was kept secret until Christ revealed it to Paul in Acts 9, which is where the Body of Christ began, with Paul.

Paul was a Roman (Gentile). Paul was of the Jewish religion. Paul's salvation exemplifies the Body of Christ: Jew and Gentile in one body.

And these people do not want you to know that because (1) they don't know it themselves,

Baloney.

(2) they move it to whatever position is convenient for them,

More baloney.

(3) they want it anywhere that *excludes* water baptism.

You can spell it bologna or baloney, it is the same thing.

> That is the teaching. The people that propagate this now are Cornelius Stam and (Sadler), who publish the *Berean Searchlight* and several commentaries. Although these people have some sound thoughts about the difference between the Petrine ministry and the Pauline ministry, when it comes to dispensational truth some (sic: he meant to say none) of them could tell you when this dispensation started if their life depended upon it.

Same old baloney served in a straw man's sandwich. Now, this next is great fun:

> I'll give you a sample of the conversation I have had with eight of them on eight different occasions through a period of twenty years.
>
> The conversations run like this:
>
> "Brother Ruckman, can you show me one verse in the Bible that commands us to be baptized in water?"
>
> Yes, I can.
>
> "Where?"
>
> Matthew 28:19, **"Go ye therefore, and teach all nations, baptizing them in the name of the Father, and of the Son, and of the Holy Ghost."**
>
> "Brother Ruckman, doctrinally that refers to the Tribulation."
>
> You mean, it may refer *dispensationally* to the Tribulation, but some things that refer to the Tribulation *can* refer to the church age.

What a hoot!

Not only is it apparent the good Doctor agrees that Matthew 28:19 is Tribulation doctrine, a fact to which almost none of Dr. Ruckman's followers would concur, Dr. Ruckman invents something called the "church age." There is no such thing as the "church age" in anybody's Bible, as we all should know.

There was an Old Testament church:
> *Acts 7:38: This is he, that was in the church in the wilderness with the angel which spake to him in the mount Sina, and with our fathers: who received the lively oracles to give unto us:*

There was Peter's church at Jerusalem:
> *Acts 2:47: Praising God, and having favour with all the people. And the Lord added to the church daily such as should be saved.*

And there is the church which is His body, that according to the revelation of the mystery:
> *Colossians 1:25-27: Whereof I am made a minister, according to the dispensation of God which is given to me for you, to fulfil the word of God; Even the mystery which hath been hid from ages and from generations, but now is made manifest to his saints: To whom God would make known what is the riches of the glory of this mystery among the Gentiles; which is Christ in you, the hope of glory:*

But back to Dr. Ruckman's purported experiences talking to us hyper-ultra-JW-SDA-like heretics. The conversation begins with the dispensationalist asking for an example of things that refer to the Tribulation also referring to the so-called church age:

"For example, what?"

I'll give you a good example. Revelation 12 says, **"They overcame"** the devil **"by the blood of the Lamb, and by the word of their testimony; and they loved not their lives unto**

the death." That's as good a "church age doctrine" as you ever found in all your life.

Well, not exactly.

We don't overcome by the final sacrifice of a Lamb which was in accordance with Israel's law program. We are not sheep, that would be Israel; and so the Lamb corresponds to being one with Israel, not one of us. That is why Paul always refers to Christ as the man.

> *1 Timothy 2:5: For there is one God, and one mediator between God and men, the man Christ Jesus;*

Not the Lamb: Christ Jesus, the man. Christ did two things on that one cross. He was the Lamb slain for Israel and the man who paid for the sins of those who hated him.

Remember, every verse in the Bible has three applications: historical, spiritual and doctrinal. What Dr. Ruckman does in his illustration is to disregard the verse's historical and doctrinal settings, which is shameful workmanship. The doctrine in the verse requires enduring unto the end and overcoming by saying words in addition to the application of Israel's blood sacrifice. Using a Tribulation verse in that manner creates more problems than it solves and leads to the kind of confusion that is apparent among most church-going people.

At this point, Dr. Ruckman moves his illustration to arguing over water baptism:

> "Yes, but you know this can't be dispensationally true here because in the Book of Acts they didn't baptize in the name of the Father, Son and Holy Ghost. They baptized in the name of *Jesus*.
>
> No, you missed a statement in Acts 10 where they were baptized in the *name of the Lord.*
>
> "Well, that was the name of Jesus."

While the conversation above is, admittedly, pointless, we do see from it that Dr. Ruckman seems to have a water fixation.

Time to sing a good ol' Baptist hymn: "There is power, power, power in the tub, in the tub of the Lamb"

Because without being baptized you can't teach or preach in any Baptist church. You can't join the choir or serve as treasurer or secretary: not without the power of the tub. You can't serve communion, you can't take communion. There is only one thing a person who has not been baptized is allowed to do in any and every Baptist church: you are allowed to tithe.

> No, you missed it again. Matthew 28 says to baptize in the *name* of the Father, Son and Holy Ghost. Cornelius in Acts 10 was a *Gentile*.

What is really interesting here is that Dr. Ruckman has missed that Cornelius was baptized into Peter's Jewish outfit and not into Paul's, in which there is neither Jew nor Greek.

And only a person with a baptism fixation would care what name or names was/were said or whether it was sprinkling or pouring or immersing or frontwards or backwards or how deep the water was.

Meanwhile, back to Dr. Ruckman's made up supposed composite conversation with us poor confused hyper-ultra-JW-SDA-like heretics.

> "Well, Brother Ruckman, can you give a verse in the Pauline epistles that commands water baptism?"

Why, sure.

> "What?"

First Corinthians 11:1, **"Be ye followers of me, even as I also am of Christ."**

> "Now, Brother Ruckman, you know that Paul's baptism in

the Book of Acts was a Jewish proselyte baptism of Ananias and you shouldn't follow that."

No, you're wrong. I'm not told to follow the guy that baptized Paul. *I'm told to follow Paul.* We should follow Paul's practice. *Paul was baptized.*

Yes, Paul was baptized. He was also circumcised and yet:

> *Galatians 6:14: But God forbid that I should glory, save in the cross of our Lord Jesus Christ, by whom the world is crucified unto me, and I unto the world.*

And the point of following Paul as he followed Christ would be exactly that and not following Christ where Paul tells us we should not. Paul learns from Christ that in this dispensation there is but one baptism and that it is not water:

> *Ephesians 4:5: One Lord, one faith, one baptism,*

> *Romans 6:3-4: Know ye not, that so many of us as were baptized into Jesus Christ were baptized into his death? Therefore we are buried with him by baptism into death: that like as Christ was raised up from the dead by the glory of the Father, even so we also should walk in newness of life.*

> *1 Corinthians 12:13: For by one Spirit are we all baptized into one body, whether we be Jews or Gentiles, whether we be bond or free; and have been all made to drink into one Spirit.*

At which point Dr. Ruckman puts words in the mouth of the hypothetical dispensationalist which are most unlikely for anyone but an Acts 28er:

> … But under a different dispensation in Acts 9."

We who are mid-Acts dispensational and know the Body of Christ began with Paul in Acts 9 would not make this statement and we would argue against those who lean toward or hold the Acts 28 position even more vociferously that does Dr. Ruckman.

Acts 2 is wrong. Acts 28 is wrong. Mid-Acts is right. Again, Dr. Ruckman is painting all dispensationalists with the same brush, which is a wrong thing to do. Or, better said, Dr. Ruckman is trying to squeeze all dispensationalists into one bucket so that he can then kick the whole bucket into obscurity.

> Oh, I don't know about that. He is baptizing his converts in Acts 16. Someone is in trouble.

Although we have already dealt with the fact that Paul did baptize some people, it is no doubt good to repeat that it really doesn't matter. Christ sent him not to baptize. It would not matter if Paul had baptized the Green Bay Packers and Paris Hilton: Christ had not sent him to do that.

> So, when these fellows come in, they always come in like that. And finally they will come out and say, "Well, Brother Ruckman, we just don't believe water baptism is for *the church age.*" And when they say that, you ask them when this age started and I'll bet you a dollar to a doughnut that fellow will talk fifteen minutes without saying anything after you ask him that question.

The Body of Christ began with Paul in Acts 9. Take the dollar you just lost and buy yourself some donuts.

> He will quote Ephesians 2. He will quote Ephesians 3. He will run around in the Book of Acts. He will run over to Romans, He will spend that time demonstrating his great proficiency in the scriptures, but there is something he will not tell you. *He will not tell you when the church age started.*

There ain't no such thing as the Church age. A dispensation describes how God dispenses, not a period of time. Meanwhile, the Body of Christ was in the mind of God before the world began, was kept secret until Christ revealed it to Paul, and Paul was the first in the Body of Christ in this the dispensation of God's grace which is according to the revelation of the mystery.

Good night: how many times do we have to answer the same silly question?

> I said to one of these fellows one time, 'When did this age start?" After forty minutes he admitted that *he didn't know*.

Well then, you were talking to the wrong person. And I must grant you that we have no shortage of mid-Acts dispensationalists who are not well versed in the scripture. Why use them to represent all dispensationalists? Answer: so you can win the made up straw man argument. We are on to you, Doc.

> And I said, "Well, you crazy fool, what are you doing telling my people that water baptism is not for *this age* when you don't even know when this age *started?"* That is like a man saying the animals couldn't get in the ark because the ark was too small and you ask the man how big the ark was and the fool doesn't even know. That is the kind of thing you are dealing with when you are dealing with a hyper-dispensationalist. And if you want to pin the man right down, you pin him down with *where did the Body of Christ start?*

The ark was right at 699 feet long and 115 feet wide, 70 feet tall and that would approximate 3,600,000 square feet. Genesis 6 could not be any more clear, particularly when you know the size of a cubit as you find it in Ezekiel 41:8 and all through Ezekiel 43.

And the animals did not get on the ark "two by two."

> *Genesis 7:1-3: And the LORD said unto Noah, Come thou and all thy house into the ark; for thee have I seen righteous before me in this generation. Of every clean*

> *beast thou shalt take to thee by sevens, the male and his female: and of beasts that are not clean by two, the male and his female. Of fowls also of the air by sevens, the male and the female; to keep seed alive upon the face of all the earth.*

Anything else you want to know, Dr. Smarty Pants?

Oh, yes: one more time. The Body of Christ began with Paul in Acts 9.

> The next problem we have with these track runners is that if you ever convince them that the "Body" starts in Acts 2, they will say, "Then we have to have tongues like Acts 2. We have to share our property like Acts 2. Why don't we follow Acts 2 practice?"

That would seem reasonable...

> The answer to that is very simple. We don't follow Acts 2 *practice* because in Acts 2 when the events took place we had not had the full revelation and Simon Peter, who speaks, doesn't know what is going on *doctrinally*. That is the answer to that.

Now that's funny.

Dr. Ruckman blasts the ultra hyper whatever for believing in a gradual transition and he calls such thinking baloney, but clearly it is his baloney. It is the classic "pot calling the kettle black."

> There is no indication that Simon Peter knows all the truths of the New Testament in Acts 2 when he preaches. He is going by the light he has and with the light he has he is pointing to the truth. He is preaching just to Israel. He is preaching that you have to be baptized in water to receive the Holy Ghost. And, of course, in that case it is true. Later, it is not true. You say, "How do you know that later it is not?" Because we are plainly told in Acts 10 that while Simon Peter was preaching **...the Holy Ghost fell on all them which heard the word."** They didn't have to get baptized to get the Holy Ghost. They got the Holy Ghost *before* they were baptized. That is why the Church of Christ preacher will never read the Book of Acts. You will find him stopped in Acts 2 every time

and subjecting the whole Bible to Acts 2, because in Acts 10 they didn't have to be baptized in water to receive the Holy Ghost.

Now the point of Dr. Ruckman's booklet is to prove dispensationalism to be wrong; but in the paragraph above, he actually makes several dispensational points and happens to be right.

Peter is preaching only to Israel, just as he had been instructed:

> *Matthew 10:5-6: These twelve Jesus sent forth, and commanded them, saying, Go not into the way of the Gentiles, and into any city of the Samaritans enter ye not: But go rather to the lost sheep of the house of Israel.*

Peter does preach baptism, just as John the Baptist had done:

> *Mark 1:4: John did baptize in the wilderness, and preach the baptism of repentance for the remission of sins.*

> *John 1:30-31: This is he of whom I said, After me cometh a man which is preferred before me: for he was before me. And I knew him not: but that he should be made manifest to Israel, therefore am I come baptizing with water.*

Peter does not believe that Cornelius would be acceptable, which was the point of the vision of the unclean animals being declared clean, after which Peter goes away doubting. Tongues are for a sign, and Jews like Peter require a sign; and so when Cornelius speaks in tongues it is for Peter's benefit.

Not only that, where is Dr. Ruckman's answer to the hypothetical questions Dr. Ruckman asked himself:

> "Then we have to have tongues like Acts 2. We have to

share our property like Acts 2. Why don't we follow Acts 2 practice?"

What a hoot! Well, "hasta-la-shondi" dear brother, and send me some money so as to even things out.

So, these dispensationalists cannot tell you where the church age starts, but if you ever convince him that it starts at a certain place he will get rid of it by saying, "Why don't we then *practice* what they practiced back then?" The answer is because we have an advanced revelation.

And it is called the revelation of the mystery and it is comprised of information hidden since the world began as opposed to information spoken by the mouth of all the holy prophets since the world began.

And if there weren't a buck in it or if your reputation did not depend on being a drycleaner-bashing Baptist, you might have the scales fall from your eyes. But no, the Doctor persists:

> Now, once you say *that* (I mean, these fellows are all alike. A toad frog has more sense. You can't predict which way a toad frog will jump, but you can predict which way these fellows will jump every time.)

No, we are not all alike. There are mid-Acts people such as myself declaring that the Body of Christ began with Paul in Acts 9. And Dr. Ruckman has already identified that there are and have been other positions: he said O'Hair was Acts 18 and Bullinger 28. We are not all alike; and it is intellectually dishonest to be this far into his booklet and to say that we are.

But there is method to this madness: if Dr. Ruckman can fool his reader into thinking that we are all basically the same and put words most of us would never say into our mouths, he will keep his followers from studying on their own and perhaps learning the truth of the matter.

His anger concerning the dispensational people who were nasty to him and who split his church all those years ago: his anger doth eat as a canker. Frankly, having now met some of the mid-Acts men involved in Dr. Ruckman's church split, I can agree: some of them are absolute jerks; but it is time to move on and to deal with doctrine and not personalities.

> ...they will say, "Well, Ephesians 4 is an advanced revelation about 'one Spirit' that Paul didn't have when be baptized his converts and so, therefore, we shouldn't do it anymore." That is their answer. Of course, all this is simply nonsense. If Paul knew perfectly well that he had done wrong in baptizing people with water, *don't you know there would have been a whole chapter devoted to it?*

But Paul does correct himself; and although he does not take a whole chapter to do so, clearly his view of water baptism has changed:

> *1 Corinthians 1:14: I thank God that I baptized none of you, but Crispus and Gaius;*

> *1 Corinthians 1:17: For Christ sent me not to baptize, but to preach the gospel: not with wisdom of words, lest the cross of Christ should be made of none effect.*

For Paul to say there is one baptism when there are 12 different kinds of baptism in the Bible makes it clear. For Paul to speak of the Spirit baptizing the believer into the Body of Christ makes it clear.

Now, if you have a few thousand dollars invested in your baptistry, the water heater and the sign over the door, it may be more difficult; but that is not the dispensationalist's problem. As stated earlier, water baptism is not our problem.

Try this:

> *Matthew 3:11: I indeed baptize you with water unto repentance: but he that*

cometh after me is mightier than I, whose shoes I am not worthy to bear: he shall baptize you with the Holy Ghost, and with fire:

John says he baptized with water.
John says Jesus will baptize with fire.
John says Jesus will baptize with the Holy Ghost.
Paul says the Holy Ghost baptizes the believer into Christ.
Four different baptisms, but only one matters to those who would preach Christ according to the revelation of the mystery, and that is the last one, performed by the operation of God.

Colossians 2:12: Buried with him in baptism, wherein also ye are risen with him through the faith of the operation of God, who hath raised him from the dead.

For example, did you notice the difference in Simon Peter in Acts 11 when he found out that he had been wrong in telling the people they had to be baptized in water to get the Holy Ghost? Why, when Peter rehearses the matter he says in Acts 11:15-18, **"And as I began to speak, the Holy Ghost fell on them, as on us at the beginning. Then remembered I the word of the Lord, how that he said, John indeed baptized with water; but ye shall be baptized with the Holy Ghost. Forasmuch then as God gave them the like gift as he did unto us, who believed on the Lord Jesus Christ; what was I, that I could withstand God? When they heard these things, they held their peace and glorified God, saying, Then hath God also to the Gentiles granted repentance unto life."** When Simon Peter found out that a man *didn't have to be baptized in water* to receive the Holy Ghost, he explained it, made a speech on it, rehearsed it, gave it to the brethren, and then made a final declarative statement on it in Acts 15:11, **"But we believe that through the grace of the Lord Jesus Christ we shall be saved, even as they."**

What makes you think Paul would have done any differently if he had found out that it was wrong to baptize converts in water?

One might say that Dr. Ruckman is rather bodacious to suggest he knows what Paul would have or should have said, but you would not say that if you have ever listened to Dr. Ruckman's ad lib Bible commentary.

Rather than supposing, we will limit ourselves to the Bible we do have rather than wishing for the Bible we don't have. And in the Bible we do have it is clear that Paul disparages water baptism, as we have already seen:

> *1 Corinthians 1:14: I thank God that I baptized none of you, but Crispus and Gaius;*

> *1 Corinthians 1:18: For the preaching of the cross is to them that perish foolishness; but unto us which are saved it is the power of God.*

To hint at this, these track runners run around the track to I Corinthians and say, **"For Christ sent me not to baptize, but to preach the gospel,"** *which is not in the Bible.* You say, "Yes it is." *No, it is not.*

I only quoted half the verse and I also left out the context.

You see, these people are all alike.

The man who will stand up and say, **"For Christ sent me not to baptize, but to preach the gospel,"** if he were a Campbellite would say, "Baptism doth also now save us." These people are all the same people and the same crowd. The context of I Corinthians 1:17, **"For Christ sent me not to baptize, but to preach the gospel,"** has nothing at all to do with the doing away of water baptism because of any advanced revelation at all. The context, verses 14, 15, 16, 17, is plainly dealing with arguments of people about who baptized them, and Paul was thanking God that he hadn't been responsible for that lest they claim him against the rest. Look at verse 13. And that isn't all. Right in the context it says that he *baptized* Crispus and Gaius and the household of Stephanas and some more whose names he had forgotten.

This is very typical of the heretic, taking the text out of the context. From these verses the great superstructure that Cornelius Stam has put up has been erected. It is a superstructure that says that the eleven apostles of Matthew 28 were sent *just* to baptize (which is not the truth) and that Paul is not sent to baptize *at all* (which is not the truth either). The truth of the matter is that even though Paul was not sent *primarily* to baptize, he *did* baptize his converts. Why would he be sent primarily to baptize anyway when he wasn't a *pastor* and didn't have a local congregation? He was a traveling evangelist.

It is *not* true that the apostles were sent just to baptize. They went sent to baptize, *to preach* the remission of sins, *to teach* all nations and to be *witnesses* unto Jesus Christ (Acts 1). So, this is how you get people into trouble. You just give them part of the truth and you don't give them all the truth.

This from a man who is quick to point out how wrong it is to add words to or delete words from the text of our King James Bible: the word "primarily" comes to us from Pensacola, not from the Holy Ghost. Having said that, let us look at the context and see if the premise of this argument holds water.

1 Corinthians 1:13: Is Christ divided? was Paul crucified for you? or were ye baptized in the name of Paul?

The issue in the context is Christ: not crucifixion or baptism. To maintain that this verse proves water baptism would be to claim that it also proves crucifixion, but no one is suggesting that.

1 Corinthians 1:14: I thank God that I baptized none of you, but Crispus and Gaius;

While it is clear Paul did baptize two people it is also clear that he thanks God that he did not baptize some other people. Either baptism is not as important as it had once been or else Paul is being a spiteful jerk.

> *1 Corinthians 1:15: Lest any should say that I had baptized in mine own name.*

And we do know that the issue for unbelieving Israel was the name of the Messiah:

> *John 20:31: But these are written, that ye might believe that Jesus is the Christ, the Son of God; and that believing ye might have life through his name.*

> *Acts 4:12: Neither is there salvation in any other: for there is none other name under heaven given among men, whereby we must be saved.*

The issue is Christ, not baptism.

> *1 Corinthians 1:16: And I baptized also the household of Stephanas: besides, I know not whether I baptized any other.*

What Paul? No certificates suitable from framing? Water baptism clearly did not matter to Paul and he is pointing his audience toward Christ.

> *1 Corinthians 1:17: For Christ sent me not to baptize, but to preach the gospel: not with wisdom of words, lest the cross of Christ should be made of none effect.*

Not with wisdom of words: "May we have every head bowed (a lie), with no one looking around (another lie), and may I ask you to invite Jesus into your heart (not the gospel) and come down to this old fashioned altar (which you bought last year with the money from the bazaar) and turn from your sins (which would be works) and make Jesus lord of your life.

Then the unsaved victim of the invitation system is told that to "follow Christ" he needs to follow Christ in water baptism and he goes into the tank an unsaved dry sinner and comes out an unsaved wet sinner; but now he is qualified to take communion and later on to be a deacon.

These foolish pulpiteers don't even know that Christ was baptized twice and that they are having people follow Christ in the wrong baptism!

Christ was baptized in water to identify with Israel's ceremonial washing; but several chapters later, Christ speaks about His second baptism:

> *Matthew 20:22-23: But Jesus answered and said, Ye know not what ye ask. Are ye able to drink of the cup that I shall drink of, and to be baptized with the baptism that I am baptized with? They say unto him, We are able. And he saith unto them, Ye shall drink indeed of my cup, and be baptized with the baptism that I am baptized with: but to sit on my right hand, and on my left, is not mine to give, but it shall be given to them for whom it is prepared of my Father.*

> *Luke 12:50: But I have a baptism to be baptized with; and how am I straitened till it be accomplished!*

> *Mark 10:38-39: But Jesus said unto them, Ye know not what ye ask: can ye drink of the cup that I drink of? and be baptized with the baptism that I am baptized with? And they said unto him, We can. And Jesus said unto them, Ye shall indeed drink of the cup that I drink of; and with the baptism that I am baptized withal shall ye be baptized:*

Does not Romans 6 make it clear that we are baptized into His death? We dispensationalists know that Christ did not drown and we know that the word "baptism" is defined by its context, even though Dr. Ruckman accuses us of disregarding the context:

> *Romans 6:3-4: Know ye not, that so many of us as were baptized into Jesus Christ were baptized into his death? Therefore we are buried with him by baptism into death: that like as Christ was raised up from the dead by the glory of the Father, even so we also should walk in newness of life.*

So, for all Dr. Ruckman's fussing and fuming, there is no problem whatsoever with what Paul said or didn't say because, at the end of the day, water baptism is not our problem: we don't perform it. Meanwhile, a ceremony that takes about ten seconds and makes a show of the flesh is the centerpiece and focal point of tens of thousands of church auditoriums.

> Now we're right back at the question again. *Where did the Body of Christ begin?*

This just doesn't get old for him, does it?

> If the Body begins in Acts 28, you couldn't find a verse to prove anybody ought to be baptized in water. Of course, you would still have a problem because the mystery was given to Paul, *and Paul was baptized in water.* If the Body of Christ didn't begin until Acts 28, *then Paul wasn't in the Body which was revealed to him for nearly thirty years of his lifetime.* Now that's a "stroke," isn't it? That isn't all! If the Body doesn't begin until Acts 18, Paul wasn't in *the Body for about ten years of his lifetime.* When did he get in the Body? He said, **"For by one Spirit are we all baptized into one body...."** *When* did the Spirit baptize Paul into the Body of Christ? You see, the thing is nebulous and goes on and on and on.

There are some followers of Bullinger and Welch who take the Acts 28 position, and while I personally have never met a person who takes the Acts 18 position: who really cares? Dr. Ruckman is simply wrong to evaluate all dispensationalism, specifically mid-Acts dispensationalism, using other positions. But that is exactly what he is doing, knowing full well that the very man he mentions, Cornelius Stam, was mid-Acts and not Acts 18 or 28. To give you a feel for it, what Dr. Ruckman is doing is every bit as wrong as it would be to evaluate all Baptists by a combination of the Free Will Baptists, the Southern Baptists, the National Baptists, the Progressive Baptists and the Conservative Baptists.

The "if the body" and "if Paul" and "if whatever else" in the preceding paragraph is nothing but setting up a hypothetical straw dummy for the purpose of knocking him down, as if Jennifer Lopez had knocked out Mohamed Ali.

> I am going to take you through Ephesians 2 and 3 and show you the foundation texts for hyper-dispensationalism, and then we will see if they have any validity or bearing upon the truth. In Ephesians 3 I am going to read this thing exactly as Cornelius Stam and Bullinger read it. They read it that a "thing cannot be *revealed* until it is *present*" and that if a thing is not *revealed* it is not *there*. They all vehemently deny this and yet, having dealt with these fellows through a period of years, I can tell you that there is not one of them that believes a thing can be *there* unless it is *revealed*. That will not be hard to prove in a minute.

We'll see about that in a minute, but first let's consider the premise: Christ's cross is revealed in passages such as Psalm 22 and Isaiah 53 and Zechariah 12, but until the Christ died and resurrected, the prophesies about Christ were interesting but not effectual.

Dr. Ruckman accuses certain dispensationalists, who happen to disagree with each other, of saying that if a thing is not revealed it is not present. If it is present and no one knows it because it has not been revealed, what good is that thing which is present?

We were reconciled unto God by Christ; but if that information were never revealed, its presence would be meaningless, as no one would know to trust Christ's payment for sins. Dr. Ruckman's fancy footwork and convoluted arguments just don't stand up to scrutiny.

Now I am going to read it like Stam reads it. **"For this cause I Paul, the prisoner of Jesus Christ for you Gentiles, if ye have heard of the age of the dispensation of the grace of God which is given me to you-ward."** (Eph. 3:1,2). Stam makes one *age* the "Dispensation of Grace," you see? And, of course, that isn't the sentence at all. He is talking about God *dispensing grace* to Paul. Do you see **"If ye have heard of the dispensation of the grace of God which is given me to you-ward."** He is not talking about a *period of time* where grace is operative. Why, the Bible says that "Noah found grace in the eyes of the Lord." Noah is in a dispensation of grace, if you go to divide them up. **"How that by revelation he made known unto me the mystery; (as I wrote afore in few words, Whereby, when ye read, ye may understand my knowledge in the mystery of Christ) Which in other ages was not made known unto the sons of men, as it is now revealed** (when it took place) **unto his holy apostles and prophets by the Spirit; That the Gentiles should be fellowheirs, and of the same body, and partakers of his promise in Christ by the gospel: Whereof I was made a minister, according to the gift of the grace of God given to me...** (Eph. 3:3-7). See how that matches verse? **"...Given unto me by the effectual working of his power. Unto me, who am less than the least of all saints, is this grace given..."** (vv. 7, 8). There is goes again. See?

Three times you are told that the dispensation was the *handing out of grace to Paul.* It had nothing to do with any period of time. **"...That I should preach among the Gentiles the unsearchable riches of Christ; to make all men see what is the fellowship of the mystery, which from the beginning of the world hath been hid in God."** The trouble with this reading is that somebody is confounding when the thing *took place* with the time it was *revealed.* That isn't all. Paul was writing this to the Ephesians and he was dealing with the Ephesians back in the Book of Acts in chapter 19 and chapter 20, and at this time he already knows the mystery. That isn't the worst of it. The worst of it is that 1 Corinthians (written about this time) also speaks of the "mystery" in 1 Corinthians 12. *Paul knew about the mystery before Acts 18.*

Therefore we should never confound the *revelation* of the mystery with when the thing *took place.*

Pastor Stam is not the final authority in matters of faith and practice for the mid-Acts dispensationalist: the Bible is. If, in fact, Pastor Stam defined a dispensation as a period of time, then he was wrong. A dispensation is defined by God's deals, God's dispensings, not by calendars. Noah found an instance of grace, but Noah did not live in a dispensation of grace: Noah had covenants.

And again, when a thing takes place does matter. And yes, Paul does know the mystery before Acts 28 or Acts 18 because Christ told it to Paul in Acts 9 where the Body of Christ begins. And in fairness, although a dispensation is not defined by a period of time, dispensations take place during periods of time:

> *Hebrews 1:1: God, who at sundry times and in divers manners spake in time past unto the fathers by the prophets,*

Of course, that is the basic error in all the writings of Cornelius Stam and Baker and O'Hare and the men who follow them. There are many of these followers now in every city who take the *Berean Searchlight.* I know many of these men by name. They all have the same operation. They will travel hundreds of miles to meet together and tear up Baptist doctrine and they like to slip into Baptist churches as "Bible teachers" or "students" to take people out and form new groups and then they begin to fight among themselves and break up and start other groups. That is the history of this movement. This movement is an apostate movement exactly like Seventh Day Adventism or any cult or heresy.

If there are mid-Acts dispensationalists guilty of the bad behavior that has Dr. Ruckman so angry, then shame on them. Meanwhile, to call them a cult or heretics probably speaks more to Dr. Ruckman's hurt and anger than to the reality of dispensational doctrine.

My wife and I attended a Bible conference

and went to lunch with a mid-Acts missionary, his wife, two mid-Acts pastors and their wives. My wife had a salad and I had a sandwich. One person of the other six ordered the all-you-can-eat buffet and that one person kept making trips, supplying the others. Two pastors and a missionary: stealing food. Shall we measure all mid-Acts dispensationalists by them?

My wife and I left a very big tip, so as to make up for what had been stolen, and we don't go there anymore; but we still adhere to mid-Acts Pauline dispensationalism as we find it in our King James Bible. We are not a product of Pastor Stam, or anyone else: we are King James Bible believers.

> I was talking to one of these men the night before last (a young fellow that had just got (sic) saved and who is in a Nazarene church and plays the piano and organ). He was in a position where God could use him. He could have been a great blessing, but he got hung up on some of Stam's books and "he ain't worth shootin'" any more and never will be. They never recover. I've talked to scores of them. They never recover. Once they get hung they are hung up. All they can see is "water, water everywhere and not a drop to drink." I talked to the young man about these things we are talking about right here and I asked him about fifteen times when the Body began and he never could tell me. Finally I said to him, "Well, what have I got in my pocket?" He said, "I don't know what you have got in your pocket." I said, "Then does that mean it's not there?" He said, "Oh, yes, Stam says it was in the mind of God." I said, I'm talking about something being there." He said, "Oh, yes, Stam says it was in the mind of God." I said, "I don't give a flip whether it was in the mind or out of the mind of God. What I want to know is when did it start. (Sic)" He didn't know when it started.

It started in Acts 9 when the Lord Jesus gave it to Paul, who had been separated from his mother's womb for that very moment. The fact that a piano player in a Nazarene church did not know that means precious little.

And by the way: car keys, pocket knife, nail

clipper and some change: that is what I have in my pocket, but none of those things are of any use while they are hidden away in my pocket. They must be put in their proper place for them to operate.

We Bible-believing Baptists have taught two things for many years. We have taught that the local church did not begin at Pentecost. This is perfectly clear in the passage in Matthew 16 and 18, the calling out of the twelve, and in the commissioning of this local church in Matthew 28 and Acts 1. This group has a roll of 120 names on it in Acts 1. It had a treasurer who died and was replaced in Acts 1 and Matthew 26. It had a leader who was spokesman for the group, Simon Peter, Acts 1 and 2. It was a local, called out assembly, called out and chosen by the Lord. As such, it was a Jewish church. It certainly had Jews and Gentiles in it after Pentecost. This local church became an organism. It became more than an organization at Pentecost. It became a living organism, and its members were placed in Christ by a baptism of the Holy spirit. When Paul says, "...one Spirit...one Lord, one faith, one baptism, he can only refer to the same Holy Spirit and to the same baptism that put the Pentecostal disciples, Cornelius' family, the apostle Paul himself and the Ephesians into the Body of Christ (1 Cor. 12:13).

Wow. The Jewish church of the gospels morphed into the Body of Christ with the benefits of the cross before the crucifixion took place and before anyone knew the benefits of Calvary? Wow!

At this point a roar goes up from the bleachers and these poor, deluded hypers pipe up with, "This can't be because the same phenomena didn't happen." The answer to that is ppphhhuuuutt! That is the answer to that. The Lord has all kinds of phenomena. He can do it any way He wants to. Throughout the Book of Acts He changes a dozen times. In the Book of Acts one bunch of people have to be baptized to get the Holy Ghost, Acts 2; another group get the Holy Ghost before they are baptized, Acts 10; another man is born again before he is baptized in water, Acts 9; another bunch of people believe and are saved and are baptized without receiving the Holy Ghost, Acts 8; another bunch of people get saved and get baptized and don't talk in tongues until hands are laid on them, Acts 19. For you to say that the Body of Christ couldn't' "be there" because the "phenomena" varies is the utmost of something or other when Paul said that there is "one baptism," "one body," and "one Spirit." You can't get a Body other than Christ's Body from Acts 2 to Acts 9. That would make two bodies.

From Acts 2 through Acts 9 we see Israel gathered and duly constituted to go through the Tribulation and into the Kingdom. Ezekiel 36:23 lines up with Christ's prayer in John 17:

> "And I will sanctify my great name, which was profaned among the heathen, which ye have profaned in the midst of them; and the heathen shall know that I am the LORD, saith the Lord GOD, when I shall be sanctified in you before their eyes."

Ezekiel 36:24 is the gathering of Israel on the day of Pentecost: For I will take you from among the heathen, and gather you out of all countries, and will bring you into your own land.

Ezekiel 36:25 is the ceremonial washing (baptism) of Israel: Then will I sprinkle clean water upon you, and ye shall be clean: from all your filthiness, and from all your idols, will I cleanse you.

Ezekiel 36:26 is Israel being born again: A new heart also will I give you, and a new spirit will I put within you: and I will take away the stony heart out of your flesh, and I will give you an heart of flesh.

Ezekiel 36:27 is Pentecost: And I will put my spirit within you, and cause you to walk in my statutes, and ye shall keep my judgments, and do them.

It should also be noted that the same people who had the Old Testament get the New Testament, and both testaments are associated with the law program:

> *Jeremiah 31:33: But this shall be the covenant that I will make with the house of Israel; After those days, saith the LORD, I will put my law in their inward parts, and write it in their hearts; and will be their God, and they shall be my people.*

> *Hebrews 8:10: For this is the covenant that I will make with the house of Israel after those days, saith the Lord; I will put my laws into their mind, and write them in their hearts: and I will be to them a God, and they shall be to me a people:*

While our only association with the law is as a schoolmaster:

> *Galatians 3:23-26: But before faith came, we were kept under the law, shut up unto the faith which should afterwards be revealed. Wherefore the law was our schoolmaster to bring us unto Christ, that we might be justified by faith. But after that faith is come, we are no longer under a schoolmaster. For ye are all the children of God by faith in Christ Jesus.*

> *Romans 6:14: For sin shall not have dominion over you: for ye are not under the law, but under grace.*

> *Galatians 5:1: Stand fast therefore in the liberty wherewith Christ hath made us free, and be not entangled again with the yoke of bondage.*

Blowing Up the Whole System

This brings up a point now that is going to blow the whole system to pieces.

I don't know about you, but I can hardly wait.

The point is this. Were Peter, James and John in "the Body"? Now that is the crux. If you want to mess up Stam, Baker and O'Hare to where they will never get back on their feet again, you ask them if Peter, James and John were in the Body of Christ and, if so, when did they get in. (Sic)

Actually, it is quite simple: the disciples were "in Christ" as a product of the prophetic program given to Israel involving their Messiah and an earthly kingdom.

We are "in Christ" according to the revelation of the mystery whereby we are the Body of Christ headed for heavenly places, not sitting on one of twelve tribal thrones.

The disciples were "in Christ;" but the disciples were not in the Body of Christ.

I will show you why I say this. Take your Bible and turn to John 17. Look at the words. John 17:6, "I have manifested thy name unto the men which thou gavest me out of the world...." There's Peter, James and John. "...Thine they were, and thou gavest them me; and they have kept thy word." There's Peter, James and John. Verse 9, "I pray for them: I pray not for the world, but for them which thou hast given me...." There's Peter, James and John. Verse 10, "And all mine are thine, and thine are mine; and I am glorified in them." There's Peter, James and John. Verse 14, 15, 16, 17, 18, same bunch. Now watch it. Verse 21, "That they all may be one;..." Not two, one. "...As thou, Father, art in me, and I in thee, that they also may be one in us...." How do you get two bodies and two spirits out of that? And how do you get Peter, James and John in Christ and yet not in His Body, you Campbellite? Verse 23, "I in them, and thou in me, that they may be made perfect in one...."

There are not two bodies and there are not two Spirits. The disciples are one with Christ and comprise a unity which glorifies God on Earth. The Christians today comprise a unity which glorifies God in heavenly places. When we get to the dispensation of the fullness of times, which is in our Bibles although Scofield, Darby, Bullinger and Ruckman all seemed to miss it, that which is in heaven and that which is on Earth will be combined.

> *Ephesians 1: 10: That in the dispensation of the fulness of times he might gather together in one all things in Christ, both which are in heaven, and which are on earth; even in him:*

This is the difference between a Bible-believing Baptist and a Bible-rejecting ultra-dispensationalist.

You betcha.

The Bible-believing Baptist believes that Jesus meant what He said and said what He meant;

The Bible-believing mid-Acts dispensationalist believes that Jesus meant what He said and said what He meant, to whom He was speaking.

> *Romans 15: 8: Now I say that Jesus Christ was a minister of the circumcision for the truth of God, to confirm the promises made unto the fathers:*

> *Matthew 15: 24: But he answered and said, I am not sent but unto the lost sheep of the house of Israel.*

...that He was in Peter, James and John; that Peter, James and John were going to be in Him; that this high priestly prayer was answered, and that the only place it could have been answered was at Pentecost. How could Christ have gotten into them before then? He had no "Body" for them to be in then and was sitting opposite them. He didn't come into them when He arose from the dead. He simply breathed upon them and said, "Receive ye the Holy Ghost." There is only one place where "one Spirit" could have baptized Peter, James and John into "one body" and this one body that one Spirit baptizes into is the same one mentioned in Corinthians and Ephesians; One Spirit, one body, one baptism.

Do you see the problem Dr. Ruckman and so many others have created for themselves? He only sees two things: Old Testament and New Testament. What has been missed is that the Bible contains many more than just those two things. The Old Testament doesn't even show up until you are sixty-nine chapters into your Bible, and there cannot be a New Testament until the Lord dies on Calvary's cross.

> *Hebrews 9:16-17: For where a testament is, there must also of necessity be the death of the testator. For a testament is of force after men are dead: otherwise it is of no strength at all while the testator liveth.*

Does not the error jump off the page into your cognition?

> There is only one place where "one Spirit" could have baptized Peter, James and John into "one body" and this one body that one Spirit baptizes into is the same one mentioned in Corinthians and Ephesians

At Pentecost, in Acts 2, the Holy Spirit is not baptizing anyone into anything. It is Christ who baptized those people and He baptized them with the Holy Ghost. The good Doctor can't read!

> *Matthew 3:11: I indeed baptize you with water unto repentance: but he that cometh after me is mightier than I, whose shoes I am not worthy to bear: he shall baptize you with the Holy Ghost, and with fire:*

Mark 1:8: I indeed have baptized you with water: but he shall baptize you with the Holy Ghost.

Luke 3:16: John answered, saying unto them all, I indeed baptize you with water; but one mightier than I cometh, the latchet of whose shoes I am not worthy to unloose: he shall baptize you with the Holy Ghost and with fire:

John 1:26: John answered them, saying, I baptize with water: but there standeth one among you, whom ye know not;

The Spirit baptism is not John baptizing with water.

The Spirit baptism is not Peter baptizing with water.

The Spirit baptism is not Christ baptizing with fire.

The Spirit baptism is not Christ baptizing with the Spirit.

The Spirit baptism is the Spirit baptizing the Christian into Christ:

1 Corinthians 12:13: For by one Spirit are we all baptized into one body, whether we be Jews or Gentiles, whether we be bond or free; and have been all made to drink into one Spirit.

Christ is spelled C-h-r-i-s-t. Spirit is spelled S-p-i-r-i-t. They are different entities performing different baptisms with different people with different results.

In Ephesians (when he is talking about one baptism) Paul is not talking about one baptism to the exclusion of all others as a form. He is talking about the baptism that saves. That is perfectly apparent from the context. The context of Ephesians 4 is not "break off fellowship with all the folks that get baptized in water."

Well, let's see:

Ephesians 4:4-6: There is one body, (which would be to the exclusion of all others)

and one Spirit, (which would be to the exclusion of all others)

even as ye are called in one hope of your calling; (which would be to the exclusion of all others)

One Lord,(which would be to the exclusion of all others)

one faith,(which would be to the exclusion of all others)

one baptism, (but Dr. Ruckman says this is not to the exclusion of all others because we need to keep those tanks full and those baptismal waters in a frothed up frenzy.)

One God and Father of all, (which would be to the exclusion of all others)

who is above all, and through all, and in you all. (which would be to the exclusion of all others)

Hmmmm.

> The context says, "With all lowliness and meekness, with longsuffering, forbearing one another in love; Endeavoring to keep the unity of the Spirit in the bond of peace." There is nothing in Ephesians 4 about getting together and tearing up all the churches of folks who got baptized in water. The statement there is that there is one real baptism that saves a man and it is the baptism that puts him into Christ, the Holy Spirit. You can't beat that thing with a stick.

You know what: the paragraph above surely reads like Dr. Ruckman knows he is wrong or at the very least, Dr. Ruckman is appealing for us to cut him some slack. Here he says that the one baptism that matters is not water, that the one baptism of Ephesians 4:5 would be by the Spirit into Christ, not by the guy wearing the waders into the tank of tepid, torpid water.

Bless his heart, it seems Dr. Ruckman is still smarting over his church split and his heart still breaks While I absolutely understand that, having experienced something similar, one cannot hold a grudge that engenders wrong doctrine anymore that one can form alliances at the expense of Bible truth.

> The fact that Cornelius Stam and O'Hair and Baker were too dumb to think that God couldn't use multiple means or multiple methods in manifesting things throughout the Book of Acts with the same Spirit and the same baptism is just a testimony to their infidelity and their ignorance.
>
> If Peter, James and John were not in Jesus Christ, you are not either, and neither was Paul. Do you think Christ's high priestly prayer was rejected? He prayed that prayer to the Father and said, "Father, I want to be in them and them in me and the same relationship that I am in you and you in me." That is the relationship of the "mystery Body" of Ephesians 1, 2, and 3, and don't you ever doubt it for a minute.

After blasting some people he does not like, Dr. Ruckman then blasts the very Bible he loves: Christ's high priestly prayer was not rejected and Christ's relationship with those that received Him as Messiah is sure and certain. However, to read the mystery body of Ephesians back into John 17 is pure poppycock.

John 20:9: For as yet they knew not the scripture, that he must rise again from the dead.

Three chapters after the high priestly prayer, the men "in Christ" according to their prophetic program still knew nothing of the resurrection. We, as new creatures in Christ Jesus according to the revelation of the mystery, have our position as a product of trusting Christ's death, burial and resurrection as payment for our sins.

> That is not all. Turn to Ephesians 2 and begin at verse 19– speaking now to Gentile believers, Paul says, "Now therefore ye are no more strangers and foreigners, but fellow citizens with the saints, and of the household of God; And are built upon the foundation of the apostles and prophets, Jesus Christ himself being the chief corner stone."

Yes, after all:

1 Corinthians 3: 11: For other foundation can no man lay than that is laid, which is Jesus Christ.

Peter built his kingdom church upon the foundation of Christ according to prophecy.

Paul built his heavenly church upon the foundation of Christ according to the mystery.

When Paul preaches Christ, it is not as if the Lord was born in Acts 9 and that nothing had been written about Him previously. The Christ Paul preaches is not one invented by the Liberal religionists or Oprah Winfry or your superstitious nutty uncle, He is the Christ of the scriptures.

Now the problem that underlies the error here is the failure to see that there are more than just two things in the Bible. There are the maps in the back, the concordance, (or as so many water baptized Baptists say: con-cor-din-nance), and there may even be pages showing Old Testament Prophecies about Christ fulfilled in the New Testament. And with all that, there is still a failure to see the dispensational change which takes place starting in Acts 9, ushering in a new entity that is neither Israel nor under the law: the church which is His body, according to the revelation of the mystery.

To know that the one baptism to which Paul refers is Spirit, not water, and to know that we are not under law but grace and to know that we are not Israel, yet to go on fighting the truth of mid-Acts dispensationalism is surely taking one's hurt over nasty people instigating a nasty church split a bit too far.

But leave Dr. Ruckman's personal issues out of it: do you not see the errors in the anti-dispensational positions he presents and represents? If it is not yet clear, perhaps it will clear up before long.

> Baker got in such a fit here that he found eight new different apostles out of Paul's friends and tried to prove that it was those apostles referred to in Ephesians 2, but that didn't work because in Ephesians 4:11, where "he gave some, apostles," those things took place right after the ascension. Look at Ephesians 4:9-10. That won't work at all because there are "prophets in the Body of Christ" (Eph. 4:11-12) where the "mystery Body" is mentioned. You can't beat it. The apostles were in the Body. So were the prophets. And they were not the new apostles that came up after Paul.

And the very next verse provides the answer:

> *Ephesians 4:13: Till we all come in the unity of the faith, and of the knowledge of the Son of God, unto a perfect man, unto the measure of the stature of the fulness of Christ:*

You might say "until" but the word "till" is just fine in that it tells you that what had gone on previously came to a screeching halt. This corresponds to Romans 12 and I Corinthians 12 because when the revelation of the mystery came unto the measure of the stature of the fullness of Christ, there was no longer any place for anything else.

Isn't it interesting that the good Doctor stopped one verse short of the answer to his supposed conundrum? And have we not all encountered people who avoid certain verses so as to fool the green troops?

> That won't work. Look at Ephesians 2:19-3:1, "...The apostles and prophets, Jesus Christ himself being the chief corner stone; In whom all the building fitly framed together groweth unto an holy temple in the Lord: In whom ye also are builded together for an habitation of God through the Spirit. For this cause...." When faced with these scriptures, Stam, Baker, O'Hare, Moore, Bullinger and the rest of them did a flip-flop and insisted that 19 through 22 had nothing to do with the Body. Yet Ephesians 3:1 said "For this cause," and he goes right into the revelation about the Body.

Perhaps we need to draw the man a picture:

| Peter builds according to the Prophetic program for Israel. | Paul builds according to the revelation of the mystery. |

For other foundation can no man lay than that is laid, which is Jesus Christ. I Corinthians 3:11

But that isn't the worst of it. Go back to Ephesians 2 and look at verse 11 and notice that when Paul is discussing the household of God and the habitation, the foundation of the building, he was making reference to the Body of Christ. Ephesians 2:11-15, "Wherefore remember, that ye being in time past Gentiles in the flesh, who are called Uncircumcision by that which is called the Circumcision in the flesh made by hands; That at that time ye were without Christ, being aliens from the commonwealth of Israel, and strangers from the convenant6s of promise, having no hope, and without God in the world: But now in Christ Jesus ye who sometimes were far off are made might by" What? "the blood of Christ. For he is our peace, who..." (Past tense–not when he got the Body mystery. Not when the mystery was revealed in the late Acts period. Past tense) "having abolished in his flesh the enmity, even the law of commandments...." When did he do this? Verse 16, when he died on the cross, "And that he might reconcile both unto God in one body by the cross...." Now, there is the matter. And all this nonsense about "there weren't any Gentiles in Acts 1, 2 and 3 so there couldn't be any Body there because the Body is a joint Body" is just a lot of hot air. The fact the Gentiles didn't enter that Body until they got saved in Acts 2 and in Acts 8 (the Ethiopian eunuch) and the fact that pure Gentiles who weren't Jewish proselytes didn't get into the Body until Acts 13, 14, 15 and 16 does not amount to a hill of beans. The way was made for them to get in there when Jesus Christ died on the cross, verse 16. And it was preached "to you which were afar off, and to them that were nigh." It got preached first at Jerusalem to a bunch of Jews and then to those afar off, the Gentiles, "For through him we both have access by one Spirit unto the Father."

Paul told you that the one Spirit that gave the Ephesian Gentile mystery Body people access to the Father gave the Jewish Pentecostal apostles access to the Father following the crucifixion. And there it is. You can't get around that thing if you stay up all night with a Bullingerite.

How many times will anti-dispensationalists such as Dr. Ruckman try to paint all dispensationalists with the Acts 28 brush of the Bullingerites?

How many times will anti-dispensationalists such as Dr. Ruckman fail to see that Christ baptized with the Holy Spirit at Pentecost but that now the Holy Spirit is doing the baptizing, and that into Christ's body and not Christ's earthly kingdom?

How many times will the anti-dispensationalists such as Dr. Ruckman allow the fact that they are angry at some people color their ability to read?

The answer, my friend, is blowing in the wind, the answer is blowing in the wind.

> In closing, let me say this. These people are out to destroy every Bible-believing Baptist church in this country under the pretense of being able to teach you the "deeper things of the Bible." They are bloodsuckers and leeches and I don't know of a case (of all I've known in many years of the ministry) who ever got his own church going.

One cannot help but hear his anger and to feel his pain.

> Every one of their churches is made up of members of other churches. They infiltrate Baptist churches and try to teach the people that water baptism is not for this dispensation. And there is not a single one of them that knows when this dispensation even started. When Paul got knocked down on his face in Acts 9 he said, "Lord, what wilt thou have me to do?" And anybody with any sense would immediately remember the words of a dying thief (who died without water baptism, who couldn't join a church, and who was saved by grace through faith pure and simple by believing on the Lord Jesus Christ). The fact that he believed on Jesus as the kingly Messiah instead of the exact manner later revealed in the Pauline epistles doesn't mean anything.

And here again we see that Dr. Ruckman does

note Paul had new information revealed to him. Interestingly, Dr. Ruckman uses the thief on the cross to deny dispensational distinctives exactly as does the Campbellite Church of Christ Elder that Dr. Ruckman calls a "water dog".

> When a man begins to tear up his Bible, he can wrongly divide the word of truth as well as rightly divide it. Cornelius Stam has gone so far as to say that the Ethiopian eunuch who got saved by reading Isaiah 53 was not trusting the shed blood and points out to the student that Isaiah 53 is talking about Christ dying for Israel, not Ethiopian eunuchs. To which may be answered an emphatic "ppphhhhhuuuuutt!" There is nothing to that type of Bible exegesis.

But Stam was right because there is nothing in Isaiah 53 about Christ's resurrection or the Body of Christ, and yet it is Dr. Ruckman who says that same eunuch was the first person in the Bible to get saved the same way you got saved.

> If you find these men fooling around your church and trying to proselyte your young people and holding Bible studies in the homes, then you had better be on your guard. Call your people in and have them read this book and have them check the references.

And as Rocky said to Bullwinkle: "Now for something completely different;" and as Bullwinkle said to Rocky, "Watch me pull a rabbit out of my hat."

> The truth of the matter is that the Body of Christ was formed with the death of Christ, exactly as Adam had his body formed when he slept the sleep of death and Eve was taken from his side. The fact that the Body did not begin to be built until Pentecost means absolutely nothing. The fact that that Body at first contained Jews only means absolutely nothing. It was destined to have Jews and Gentiles in it and this is the mystery that was revealed to Paul after Acts 9. The fact that it was revealed to Paul after Acts 8 has no bearing upon when it started at all. It was there years before Paul was saved. His kinsmen were "in Christ" before he was in Christ. He persecuted Christ in the person of the saints in Acts 7 and 8 because they were part of the body of Christ. This Body is called "the

church of God" in Galatians 1:13, and you are told in 1 Corinthians 10, 11 and 12 that the church of God is composed of Jew and Gentile (1 Cor. 12:13).

Boink.

The Body of Christ existed years before anybody knew about it and that doesn't matter? That must mean Dr. Ruckman thinks the gospel of the kingdom preached in the gospels is the same thing as the gospel of the grace of God which Paul alone declares. That would explain why Dr. Ruckman has said the clearest presentation of the gospel is John 1:12 which is not the gospel of the grace of God at all, but rather refers to Israel's receiving the Messiah.

If the gospel of the grace of God is what Paul says it is: the death, burial and resurrection of Christ for our sins, how could the gospel of the kingdom be the same thing, when Peter and the disciples had been preaching that since Matthew 10, while in Matthew 16 Peter attempts to prevent Christ's going to the cross?

Paul says:

> *1 Corinthians 15:1-4: Moreover, brethren, I declare unto you the gospel...*
>
> *by which also ye are saved,...*
>
> *how that Christ died for our sins according to the scriptures; And that he was buried, and that he rose again the third day according to the scriptures:*

Jesus preached the gospel of the kingdom:

> *Matthew 4:23: And Jesus went about all Galilee, teaching in their synagogues, and preaching the gospel of the kingdom, and healing all manner of sickness and all manner of disease among the people.*
>
> *Matthew 9:35: And Jesus went about*

all the cities and villages, teaching in their synagogues, and preaching the gospel of the kingdom, and healing every sickness and every disease among the people.

But as we have seen before and remind ourselves again, the disciples did not understand Calvary's cross and Peter tried to prevent it from taking place:

Matthew 16:20-22: Then charged he his disciples that they should tell no man that he was Jesus the Christ. From that time forth began Jesus to shew unto his disciples, how that he must go unto Jerusalem, and suffer many things of the elders and chief priests and scribes, and be killed, and be raised again the third day. Then Peter took him, and began to rebuke him, saying, Be it far from thee, Lord: this shall not be unto thee.

How is it that the Body of Christ could be in place years before Paul was saved when that would make the difference between the gospel of the kingdom and the gospel of the grace of God irrelevant?

How could it be that we who glory in the cross of Christ and are reconciled by that cross could be said to be in the same situation as those under the weak and beggarly elements of the law with no understanding of Christ's resurrection?

And isn't the point of Jew and Gentile being the same in one body that the Jew ceases to be a Jew, and the Gentile ceases to be a Gentile, and we all become a new creature called the Body of Christ?

1 Corinthians 1: 22: For the Jews require a sign, and the Greeks seek after wisdom:

And are not both of them wrong? Isn't the point:

1 Corinthians 1: 23: But we preach Christ crucified, unto the Jews a stumblingblock, and unto the Greeks foolishness;

You can't miss it, unless of course, you choose to.

> What has this got to do with water baptism? Just this. Even if John the Baptist's water baptism was to manifest Christ to Israel, which it was, even if Simon Peter's water baptism "for repentance" was so that God could give the Holy Spirit to Israel, even though the baptism of the Ethiopian eunuch was after he was saved by grace through faith, and even though the baptism of Paul was for purification of sin, the salient fact remains that the Author and Finisher of our faith, the Lord Jesus Christ, was baptized in water, the eleven apostles who followed Him and wrote part of your New Testament were baptized in water, and Paul was baptized in water and baptized some of his coverts in water. And there is no way out of these great plain truths.

Everything said in the preceding paragraph is absolutely true; and Dr. Ruckman is making my case, not his, in that he properly identifies the purpose of the different baptisms. Of course he wants to jump to the conclusion that since water baptism had its place at one time, it should have a place at all times. Frankly, only the Baptists care.

Read this book under water, if you want to.

Instead of taking your weekly bath on Saturday night, get baptized three times a week if you care to. It will be good for your hygiene.

Buy a convertible and drive through the car wash with your top down, if you care to. (Oh, that would be sprinkling and you don't believe in that.)

The point is, baptism is not an issue for the mid-Acts Pauline King James Bible-believing dispensationalist. But it is such a big deal to the Baptists and many others that you are not considered a member of the church without it, you can't be a missionary without it, you can't be a deacon without it. As pointed out before, the only thing you are allowed to do is tithe.

And let's think about that for just a moment:

Tithing was part of the law, and you know you are not under the law.

There were three different tithes given to Israel including one in Deuteronomy 14 that the Hebrew tither got to spend on himself, and your preacher never ever mentioned that one to you. Perhaps he is afraid you would continue to tithe, but the preacher would not be cashing your checks.

But worst of all is this:

If Israel, under the law, did not tithe: Malachi 3: 9: Ye are cursed with a curse: for ye have robbed me, even this whole nation.

Dear Reader, if you are saved by the gospel of the grace of God, you cannot be cursed with a curse in that Galatians 3:13: Christ hath redeemed us from the curse of the law, being made a curse for us: for it is written, Cursed is every one that hangeth on a tree:

And so, failing to rightly divide and failing to differentiate between the gospel of the kingdom and the gospel of the grace of God and failing to recognize prophecy is different from mystery robs you of the benefits of Christ's cross.

And so it does matter, doesn't it?

And only a saturated and sodden Baptist would think the issue is baptism: they are hyper- and ultra- immersionists, are they not?

> I don't care how swift and smooth and witty and adept you are in judging the scriptures and wresting the scriptures, you cannot beat those three great salient truths. The apostle who said, "Be ye followers of me, even as I also am of Christ," submitted to water baptism. And when Paul told a man how to get saved by grace through faith in Acts 16, he let him follow the Lord in Baptism. And although Paul was not sent primarily to baptize, he did baptize. And although he may not have given

a clear commandment in the Pauline epistles on the relation of water baptism to the Body of Christ, he certainly left the matter open and certainly set the example himself and certainly never repented of his own baptism or told anybody to repent of theirs. "All unrighteousness is sin." And if it is not right to get baptized in water, water baptism is a sin and I don't recall once (sic) place in the Pauline epistles where Paul ever confessed that "sin." However, I can turn you to five other places where he confessed a dozen sins he committed before he was saved. In his great statement after he was saved he said, "...Christ Jesus came into the world to save sinners; of whom I am chief." In his great confession of sin as a Christian in Romans 7, Paul never mentioned water baptism one time. Paul followed the Lord in baptism and rested in it content. He only taught that there was one saving baptism, that was the Holy Spirit, and that the same Spirit that put people into the Body of Christ is (sic) Acts 2 put them into the Body of Christ in Acts 8, 9, 10, 16, 18, 28 and up until the rapture of the Body of the Lord Jesus Christ. We Bible-believing Baptists don't make too much of an issue out of it because we believe that a man is saved by grace through faith and that baptism is only a figure of salvation, 1 Peter 3:21. But people who follow Cornelius Stam and the ultra-dispensationalists will always make an issue out of it. The only theme song they have is "How dry I am, how dry I am," and their teaching and preaching is as dry as their baptism.

I trust that this will be a blessing to you and that you will search the scriptures to see if these things be so.

Dr. Ruckman is certainly right about the teaching and preaching within the grace movement: most grace preachers and teachers could not stir up a bucket of paint, much less an audience. And Dr. Ruckman is certainly right when he says about us, (although he did not say it in this booklet), that no people talk more about Paul and yet no people act less like Paul when it comes to preaching, teaching and evangelism. It could well be said of the grace movement that someone needs to draw a line on the ground so we can see if it really is moving, standing still, or going backward.

But, Dr. Ruckman and so many others are just wrong when they think we make an issue out of baptism. If the anti-dispensational churches did not have the baptistry as the focal point of their auditoriums and require baptism as a requisite for being a proper Christian, we would never have even thought to bring it up.

Meanwhile, we thank our Lord for Dr. Ruckman and the many right things he has taught us all. We thank him for his being plain spoken and for taking dispensationalists to task in his booklet. After all, iron sharpeneth iron.

The Summation

And now, what follows is Dr. Ruckman's summation of the prose which preceded it. The next few pages would be great material for every mid-Acts dispensational assembly to use as part of Sunday School curriculum as we all need to be able to answer the opposition. In his summation, Dr. Ruckman is brief and to the point and we will respond in like manner.

WHAT HYPER-DISPENSATIONALISTS TEACH

1. There is a period of time called "THE GRACE OF GOD" which began in Acts 9 (Stam, Baker, Moore, Natkins (sic)) or in Acts 18 (O'Hare and others) or in Acts 28 (Bullinger, Ballinger, Greaterex).

We would say that we live in the dispensation of the grace of God which began when Christ gave the revelation of the mystery to Paul, and that a dispensation is not defined by time but rather by how God chooses to dispense His dealings with His creation.

2. Water baptism is not for "THIS AGE" since "THIS AGE" began in Acts 9 or Acts 13 or Acts 18 or Acts 28.

Water baptism is not for Christians in this dispensation as there is but one baptism in place and that by the Spirit, not by the bucket or the tub.

3. Bible-believing Baptists are heretics who do not follow "Pauline" teaching (1Tim. 1:16).

Bible-believing Baptists are sloppy, and since they are not Pauline they fail to rightly divide more often than not. Many are saved in spite of the poor quality teaching they endure.

4. Since Paul did not COMMAND anyone to be baptized, it is UNSCRIPTURAL.

Baptism by water is scriptural, one of twelve baptisms found in the Bible. We, however, are baptized by the Holy Spirit into Christ's death, and Christ did not drown.

5. Since Paul was not "SENT TO BAPTIZE," water baptism is PRE-PAULINE (1Cor. 1).

Correct: there is one baptism in this dispensation and it is not Israel's ceremonial washing.

6. The "ONE BAPTISM" of Ephesians 4 automatically cancels water baptism (Moore, Stam, Sharpe, Baker).

If there is one in the Bible, why should there be two in the church?

THE BIBLE REBUKE OF THE "HYPERS"

The "DISPENSATION" OF Ephesians 3:2 was the grace which God gave to Paul to preach (Eph. 3:7, 1 Cor. 3:10, Col 1:29). Grace was "DISPENSED" to him. The "GRACE OF GOD" is found in every period of time (Gen. 6:8. Exod. 33:13).

A dispensation is not a period of time but rather is defined by the manner with which God deals with His creation. Noah found grace, for example, before the law dispensation and apart from the grace dispensation.

2. The age of the ONE BODY and the "church of the ONE BODY" began in Matthew 27 (see Eph. 2:12, 16) with twelve apostles "IN CHRIST" (Rom. 16:7) before Paul was saved (John 17:21, 23).

At the cross (Matthew 27) there were to be 12 apostles who were to sit on 12 thrones in an earthly kingdom, ruling with their Messiah. They were "in Christ" by the prophetic program while we, who have no part of Israel's promises and covenants, are "in Christ" by the mystery program.

> 3. Paul was baptized in water (Acts 9:18) and baptized some of his converts (Acts 16:33, 18:8, 1 Cor. 1:14-16), even though he was an evangelist.

The Bible never says Paul was an evangelist but rather that Paul is the apostle to the Gentiles; and although he did baptize some people in water, the Lord brought that to a halt by sending Paul not to baptize but to preach the gospel.

> 4. Paul COMMANDED NO ONE to attend church, pass out tracts, proselyte Baptists who are already saved, or argue about water baptism.

Good point: irrelevant to the issues surrounding dispensationalism, but a good point none the less. Dr. Ruckman, if it makes you feel any better, we join you in being ashamed of the mid-Acts dispensationalists that tore up your church and that are making messes even today.

> 5. He DID baptize (1 Cor. 1:14-16) and only thanked God that people weren't baptized in his name (1 Cor. 1:14-18). Paul was not sent by Mark 16:16-18 but he is the only apostle who fulfilled that commission.

Since Paul's new dispensation of grace overlapped the fall of Israel, Paul had what the Bible calls "special signs" for unbelieving Israel in that Paul could go to unbelieving Jews subsequent to their being declared uncircumcised in heart and ears. (Acts 7:51)

> 6. The Corinthian converts who were baptized by ONE Spirit into ONE Body (1 Cor. 12:13) were baptized in water (Acts 18:8).

Correct: but that did change when Paul met with the Lord after Acts 9, after Acts 18.

THE HYPER-DISPENSATIONALIST'S PERVERSION OF EPHESIANS 4:5

1. (sic) Stam, Baker, Bullinger, Ballinger and Watkins all take Ephesians 4:4-5 out of the context in which it appears (as any Campbellite will also do) and pretend that it is talking about WATER BAPTISM being replaced by spirit baptism. This explains why 95 percent of any "Hyper" CONGREGATION are ex-Baptists.

Whatever. If the people that comprise that 95% want to leave, they have voted with their feet and there is no point crying over spilled milk. Perhaps in a grace assembly they have heard the gospel of God's grace with clarity and gotten saved. Vance Havner (Baptist preacher for over 70 years) and B. R. Lakin (Baptist preacher for over 50 years) each told me that they believed that two thirds to three quarters of the members of the average Baptist church will spend eternity in hell. Can we have every head bowed, every eye closed as we invite people to come down front and ask Jesus into their heart?

2. The context of Ephesians 4:4-6 is the unity of the Body of Christ, not "DISUNITY" caused by carnal Christians who say: "I AM OF CHRIST" (1 Cor. 1:12).

Yes, unity. He wants unity his way and I want unity my way, and neither of us is likely to compromise. Well, let's just scrap our Bibles, let's all join hands and sing: "Kum bya my Lord, Kum by aaaaa. Kum by yaaaaaa my Lord, Kum by yaaaaaaaaa."

3. The same baptism that put Paul into Christ ("WE," 1 Cor. 12:13) put Gentile believers (Corinth, Ephesus) into Christ.

Thank you, Sir: you have that exactly right, and, it ain't water.

4. The same baptism that put "THE TWELVE" into Christ (Acts 1:5) put the Roman converts into Christ (Rom. 6:1-3, 16:7).

But now you have gone too far. The very verses that Dr. Ruckman used from John 17 to demonstrate that the apostles were "in Christ" refer to the apostles being "in Christ' subsequent to the high priestly prayer of John 17. Christ would baptize them with the Holy Ghost at Pentecost; and so it was not water, even for them. Water baptism was a testimony, nothing more.

ONE BAPTISM

> Hypers teach two or three baptisms of the Spirit, although the context of ONE BAPTISM is ONE SPIRIT (Eph. 4:4, 5).
>
> There are seven baptism (Matt. 3:11, 28:11-20, Acts 2:38, Matt. 20:22, 1 Cor. 10:1-3, Eph. 4:4).
>
> There are MANY lords and gods (1 Cor. 8:5)(note: Eph. 4:5-6).

Actually, there are twelve baptisms in the Bible, but seven out of twelve is better than most Baptists who don't even know the Lord Himself was baptized twice. (Luke 12:50). And again, the many lords and many gods makes my point and there is only one Lord and one God that would be the right Lord and the right God: yes, there are twelve baptisms in the Bible, but only one is right for now.

FALSE TEACHINGS OF HYPER-DISPENSATIONALISTS

> 1. PETER AND PAUL PREACHED "DIFFERENT" GOSPELS. If they did then Peter was cursed (Gal. 1:8-9). God taught Peter the Gospel in Acts 10:43, which he publicly acknowledges in Acts 15:11, while ALL ARE PRASTICING (sic) WATER BAPTISM.

We have already seen that Peter was preaching the gospel of the kingdom starting in Matthew 10 and six chapters later attempts to stop Christ from going to the cross. The cross is the central element of the gospel of the grace of God; and so it is not possible that Peter and Paul preached the same message. In Acts 10:43 Peter continues to talk of Christ's name, not Christ's death, burial and resurrection. In Acts 15:11, Israel gets grace as a product of the Messiah's sacrifice (I Peter 1:13) and we get grace as a product of our Saviour's sacrifice, (Romans 4:4-5), one prophesied, the other a mystery.

> 2. REPENTANCE SHOULD NOT BE PREACHED IN THIS AGE. Paul preached it constantly (Acts 20:21) and asked exactly what John the Baptist asked for when he preached it (Acts 26:20). Paul did this after writing Romans 16:25-26).

Works for salvation should not be preached in this dispensation; and nearly every Baptist believes that "repent" means "turn" when it does not. To ask an unsaved person to turn from his or her sins prior to salvation is even more ridiculous that asking the frog to turn into the handsome price without having been kissed by the beautiful princess: it just can't happen. The word "repentance" in both Greek and English means to have a change of mind.

> 3. THE "BODY" COULD NOT HAVE BEEN AT PENTECOST BECAUSE NO ONE MENTIONED IT. Neither did any one mention the complete abolition of the Law (Levitical) or the fulfilling of the Law (Acts 13:38-40) though both (Col. 2:14-16) were accomplished FACTS (Gal. 3:13).

The Body of Christ is made possible by the cross; but at the cross and all the way until the Lord comes to Paul in Acts 9, every word is directed to Israel, and that according to Israel's prophetic program.

> 4. MATTHEW 28:19-20 IS LIMITED TO THE TRIBULATION. Pure conjecture (see 1 Tim. 6:3, written to saints in "THE ONE BODY). (sic) The "ALL THINGS" of Matthew 28:20 does not include all PRE-CRUCIFIXION instruction, which is apparent to anyone by comparing Matthew 10:1-10 with Matthew 28:19-20 and John 13-17.

The Tribulation had NOT begun in 33 A. D. Note: "UNTO THE END OF THE WORLD."

To agree with the premise of this argument we need to buy a bottle of "White Out" and cover Acts 2:16-17 because apparently Peter was mistaken. Meanwhile, note how cleverly Dr. Ruckman has rid himself of following the pre-resurrection "all things;" and would not one of those "all things" be water baptism?

> 5. PAUL WAS DECEIVED ABOUT WATER BAPTISM AND THE "ONE BODY" UNTIL HE WROTE EPHESIANS 3-4 (after Acts 28).
>
> Then he sinned against God in not confessing it.

You know what? Our sins are forgiven without confessing them. We do not need the so-called "Christian bar of soap" found in First John 1:9 when we know that Christ paid for all of our sins with His shed blood. Paul had no need to confess to get forgiveness; Paul simply needed to stop water baptizing per the instructions Paul received from Christ; and that is exactly what happened.

> He sinned against YOU in not telling you straight out in plain clear-cut commands (note 1 Thess. 5 and Rom. 14) not to make the same mistake.

What could be more clear than what Paul did in fact write in 1 Corinthians 1, verses 14 and 18? But perhaps Dr. Ruckman's requirement that Paul make a bigger deal of it is a product of the fact that Dr. Ruckman's dedication to a tank of warm water underneath the pretty picture he painted has made baptism so inordinately important.

> Every Christian leader in the New Testament was baptized in water: none of them "REPENTED" of such an action.

So-ever-what?

The real point must be that we are not in the New Testament, we do not get our gospel from the New Testament, and if you followed New Testament doctrine to the letter, you would end up in hell with a burning Bible in your hands there to remind you that you cannot mix law and grace, you cannot mix faith with works. (Romans 11:6)

Dr. C. I. Scofield, in his reference Bible, says in his note on page 1252:

"In his (Paul's) writings alone we find the doctrine, position, walk, and destiny of the church;" and he said that back in 1917. Funny thing: Dr. Ruckman has more than once complained that Baptists are stuck in the mud right where Scofield left them in 1917, when Dr. Ruckman himself has missed what Scofield had right all those years ago.

Study to shew thyself approved unto God, a workman that needeth not to be ashamed, rightly dividing the word of truth.

- 2 Timothy 2:15

Epilogue

And so there you have it: mid-Acts dispensationalism was shot at by one of the best, and missed.

Dr. Ruckman loves his hockey and played well into his eighties; and in his booklet, <u>Hyperdispensationalism</u>, he delivers some well aimed slap shots and some pretty good body checks. We will always be thankful, more than most, for Dr. Ruckman's good humor and for his staunch defense of God's perfectly preserved words in our King James Bible.

Dr. Ruckman's style is an acquired taste and not for the babe nor the faint of heart; and while disagreeing with his booklet, and while answering his sarcasm with sarcasm, we do not disrespect the man: we take issue with his Baptist doctrine.

Since the booklet <u>Hyperdispensationalism</u> does such an excellent job of attacking dispensational doctrines, it is hoped this book, <u>Shot At And Missed</u> will provide answers to those new to dispensationalism who need some help responding to critics.

Ultimately, whether you, Dear Reader, are a Baptist or mid-Act dispensationalist or something else altogether, you must:

Romans 14:5 ... Let every man be fully persuaded in his own mind.

Every edition of Dr. Ruckman's newsletter contains what he calls "The Creed Of The Alexandrian Cult." Although we may disagree on dispensationalism, it is with respect and total agreement that we offer Dr. Peter S. Ruckman's most insightful creed:

THE CREED OF THE ALEXANDRIAN CULT

1. There Is **no final authority** but God.

2. Since God Is a Spirit, there Is **no final authority** that can be seen, heard, read, felt, or handled.

3. Since all books are material, there is **no book on this earth that is the final and absolute authority** on what is right and what is wrong: what constitutes truth and what constitutes error.

4. There **WAS** a series of writings one time which, **IF** they had all been put into a BOOK as soon as they were written the first time, **WOULD HAVE** constituted an infallible and final authority by which to judge truth and error.

5. However, this series of writings was lost, and the God Who inspired them was **unable to preserve their content** through Bible-believing Christians at Antioch (Syria), where the first Bible teachers were (Acts 13:1), and where the first missionary trip originated (Acts 13:1-52), and where the word "Christian'" originated (Acts 11:26).

6. So, God chose to **ALMOST** preserve them through Gnostics and philosophers from Alexandria, Egypt, even though God called His Son OUT of Egypt (Matthew 2), Jacob OUT of Egypt (Genesis 49), Israel OUT of Egypt (Exodus 15), and Joseph's bones OUT of Egypt. (Exodus 13).

7. So, there are two streams of Bibles: the most accurate --

- though of course there is **no final, absolute authority** for determining truth and error: It is a matter of "preference"---are the Egyptian translations from Alexandria. Egypt. which are "almost the originals" although not quite.

8. The most **inaccurate translations** are those that brought about the German Reformation (Luther, Zwingli, Boehler, Zinzendorf, Spencer, etc.) and the worldwide missionary movement of the English-speaking people: the Bible that Sunday, Torrey Moody, Finney, Spurgeon, Whitefield, Wesley, and Chapman used.

9. But we can "tolerate" these if those who believe in them will tolerate US. After all, since there is **NO ABSOLUTE AND FINAL AUTHORITY** that anyone can read, teach, preach. or handle, the whole thing is a matter of "PREFERENCE." You may prefer what you prefer, and we will prefer what we prefer; let us live In peace, and if we cannot agree on anything or everything, let us all agree on one thing: **THERE IS NO FINAL, ABSOLUTE, WRITTEN AUTHORITY OF GOD ANYWHERE ON PLANET EARTH.**

This is the Creed of the Alexandrian Cult

The King James Bible is God's perfect word, perfectly preserved by God without even one error.

Bible Baptist Church

BIBLICAL — PRE-MILLENNIAL — MISSIONARY — INDEPENDENT

Dr. Peter S. Ruckman, Pastor   Brian Donovan, Associate Pastor

March 30, 2008

Pastor Terence McLean
P. O. Box 87
Alpha, OH 45301

Dear Pastor McLean:

I got your letter requesting permission to use the booklet. The booklet on Hyper-Dispensationlism was copyrighted 1985.

The work now that is copyrighted is called "How To Teach Dispensational Truth." That is the complete thing on Hyper-Dispensationlism. If you want to use anything that is appropriate, you may do so. It is perfectly alright with me. I don't mind anybody using my stuff for anything as long as they don't pirate it and sell the stuff.

As far as quotations are concerned, you can use as many quotations from my works as you like, giving credit. Just don't make a book that contains anything but the quotations and then selling it.

Sincerely in Christ,

Peter S. Ruckman

Dr. Peter S. Ruckman
PSR:sh

Church   Located at the corner of Jo Jo and Jernigan Roads   Bookstore
(850) 476-2945   (850) 477-8812

We do thank Dr. Ruckman for his gracious permission to use "anything" from his booklet in this publication.

Dr. Peter S. Ruckman earned his Bachelor of Arts Degree from the University of Alabama and his Master of Arts and Doctor of Philosophy from Bob Jones University.

Books written by Dr. Ruckman include his Bible Believer's Commentary series with over 120 other titles in print, defending the King James Bible. Audio messages number into the thousands, including his Ad-lib Bible, illustrated messages, and verse-by-verse Bible commentaries.

Dr. Ruckman was the Pastor of the Bible Baptist Church of Pensacola, Florida, and the President and Founder of the Pensacola Bible Institute.

Literally scores of men so profited from Dr. Ruckman's teachings that those men went on to be Pastors and Missionaries.

Most biographical accounts of Dr. Ruckman include his ability to read seven hundred words per minute and his having read 6,500 books before he earned his doctorate, and about one book per day since.

Apart from his scholarly and literary attributes, however, Dr. Ruckman has a heart for souls and has seen thousands saved during his many years of ministry. His love for men in prison as well as those who collect his art and those who learned to be Bible believers are hallmarks of his preaching career.

While there are those who do not appreciate Dr. Ruckman's blunt "style," we find it to be both refreshing and Pauline: II Corinthians 11:6 But though I be rude in speech, yet not in knowledge; but we have been throughly made manifest among you in all things.

Identifying God's perfectly preserved words.

God inspired the Bible and expects us to use the Bible, which is impossible if God did not preserve His Bible. God did preserve His words perfect and without error in the King James Bible. This 90 page book about the History of Your Bible provides the proof.

Author's books on important subjects.

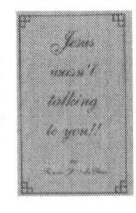

Basics of Mid-Acts, Dispensational Prayer, Jesus Wasn't Talking to You, History of Dispensational Thought, Hebrews, We are NOT Grafted In. Available at:

www.discerningthetimespublishing.com

amazon.com

Rightly dividing the red letters.

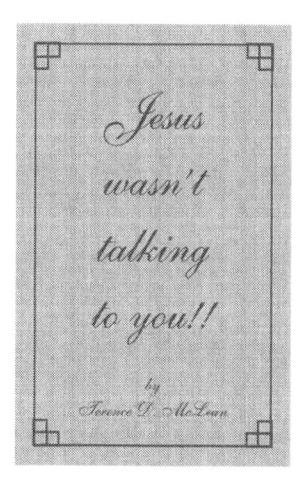

Jesus wasn't talking to you!!

by Terence D. McLean

Just because Jesus said it does not mean he said it to you. This is a great introduction to the dispensational principle of knowing the audience and where we can find our instructions from the Lord today.
(Hint: It's not in the red letters.)

Author's books on important subjects.

Basics of Mid-Acts, Dispensational Prayer, History of KJB, History of Dispensational Thought, Hebrews, We are NOT Grafted In. Available at:

www.discerningthetimespublishing.com

amazon.com

Cover the basics.

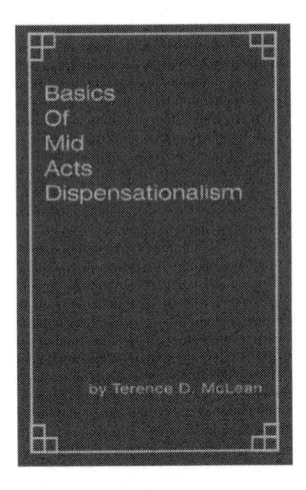

Basics Of Mid Acts Dispensationalism
by Terence D. McLean

This short 100 page book is a primer in the basic distinctions of Mid-Acts Dispensationalism. Applying these principles will open your eyes to understand the Bible like never before. A must have for anyone who wants to learn the Mid-Acts position.

Author's books on important subjects.

Jesus Wasn't Talking to You (Red Letters), Dispensational Prayer, History of KJB, History of Dispensational Thought, Hebrews, We are NOT Grafted In. Available at:

www.discerningthetimespublishing.com

amazon.com

Get Started Right.

Start Rightly Dividing:

How to start studying with the right heart from the right Bible rightly divided.

Paperback ~ 135 pages

Do you ask, 'What is right division?', 'Where do I begin?', or 'How do I start?' This short book provides the right place to start with your heart, getting the right tools, and an introduction to right division and dispensational Bible study. It ends with 33 Bible study tips for helping you do the work.

Available at:

AmbassadorsPublishing.com

amazon.com

A most important question for children.

With over 10,000 in print, this children's book communicates the gospel of grace clearly for both parents and children. Follow Patty as she asks her neighbors, "How do you go to heaven?"

These children's books are great as coloring books, bedtime stories, Sunday school lessons, and contain sound doctrine that communicates to parents, too. Available at:

www.discerningthetimespublishing.com

amazon.com